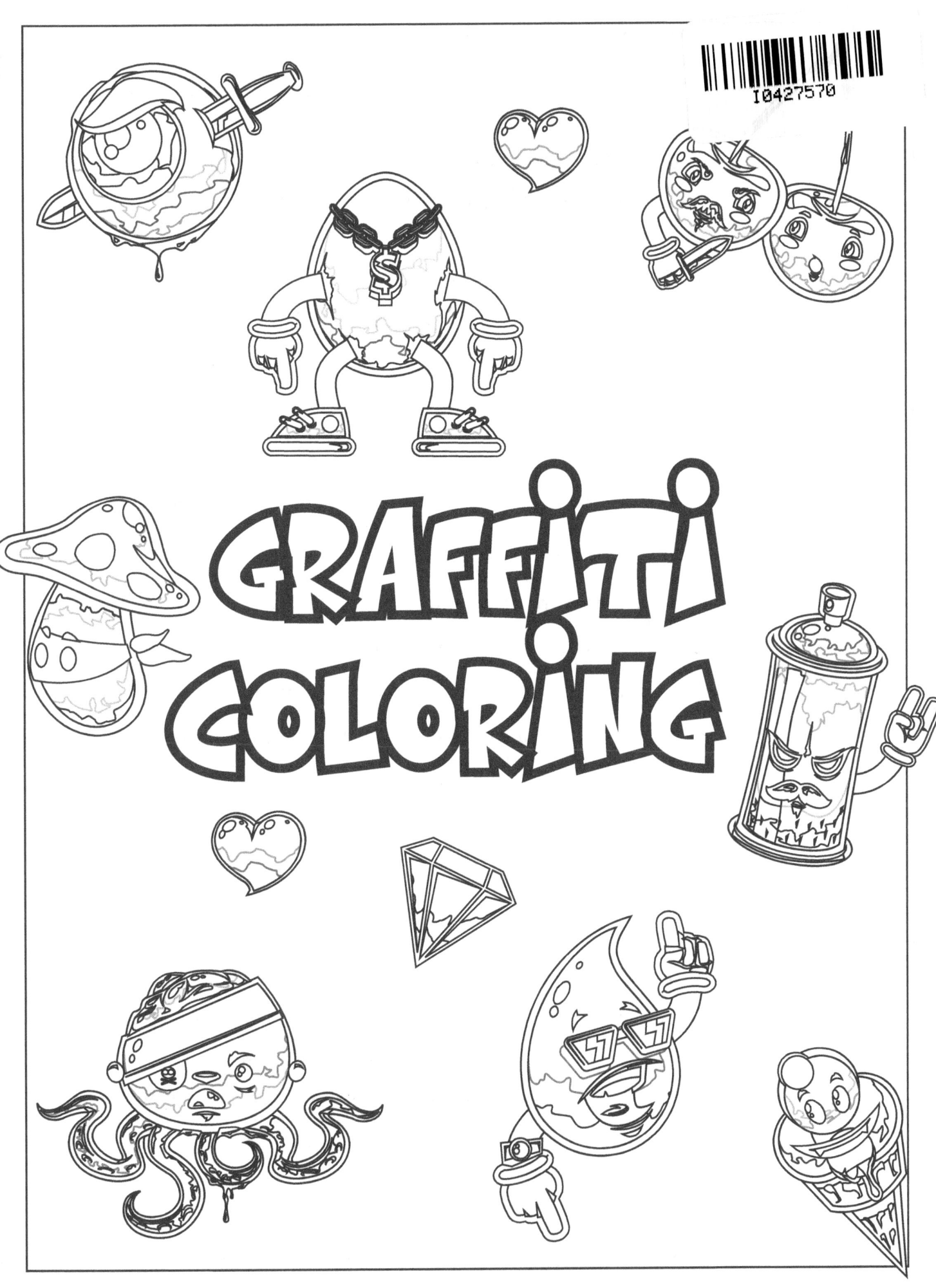

Coloring For Adults: A Childhood Pastime Turned Therapeutic Hobb

Indulge in the timeless joy of coloring, once revered as a cherished
childhood pastime now transformed into a sophisticated avenue
for relaxation and creative expression among adults
In recent years, the creative market has witnessed a surge of innovative
coloring options tailored for the discerning tastes of adults
featuring intricate themes and captivating geometric designs

Discover the enchanting allure of coloring books with sophisticated themes
where every stroke unveils a world of contentment relaxation
and overall wellness. Immerse yourself in the intricate designs
allowing your focus to transcend the mundane and transport
you to a realm where creativity flourishes

For enthusiasts, coloring becomes an immersive experience
a transformative journey that transcends the complexities of adult life
Each stroke of color is an invitation to rediscover the richness of creativity
reminiscent of the innocence found in simpler childhood days. Coloring, in its essence
offers a respite from the burdens of the adult mind, providing a fleeting escape
to a world where beauty and creativity take center stage
Elevate your coloring experience to a new level of sophistication and artistic expression

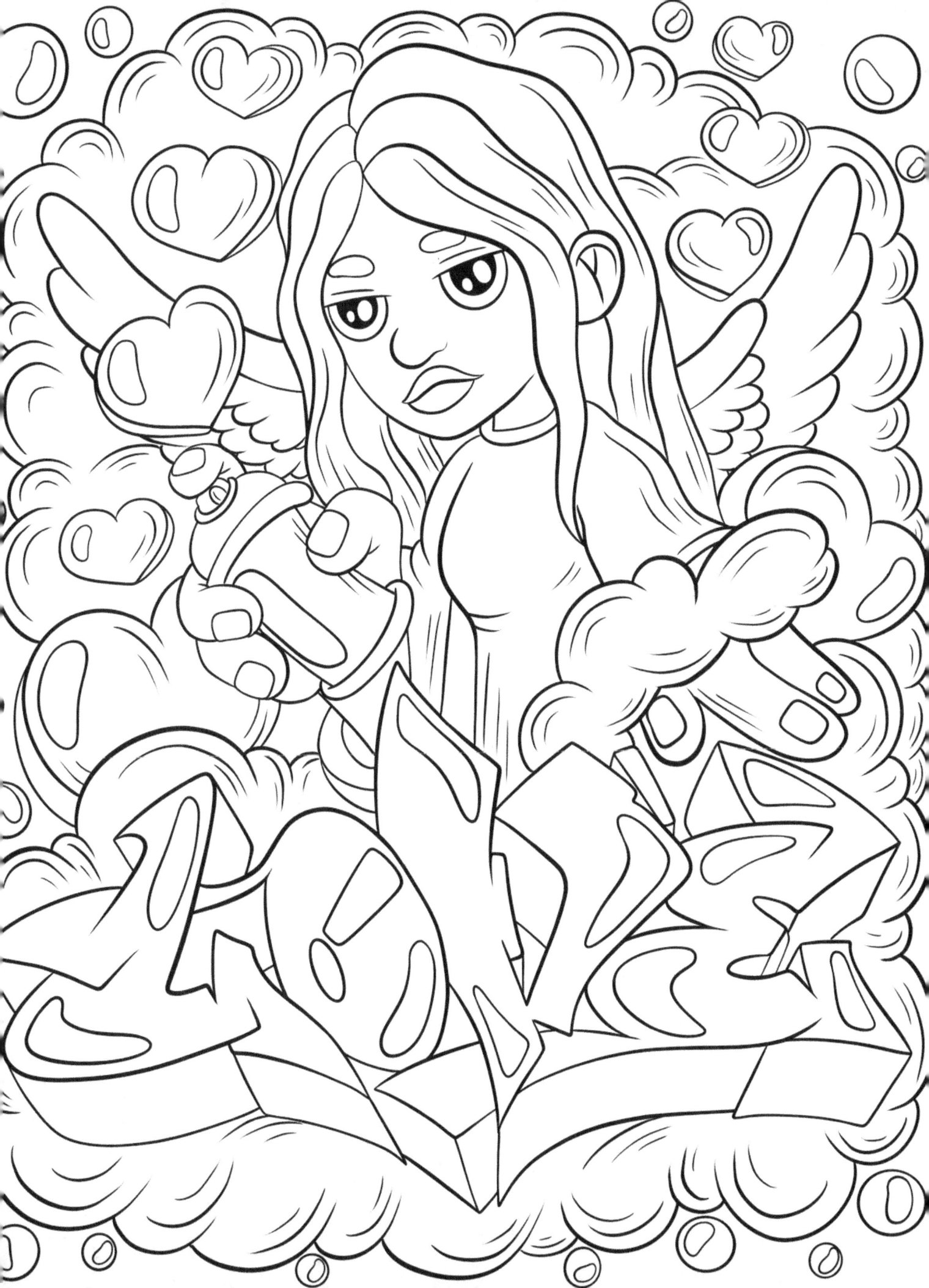

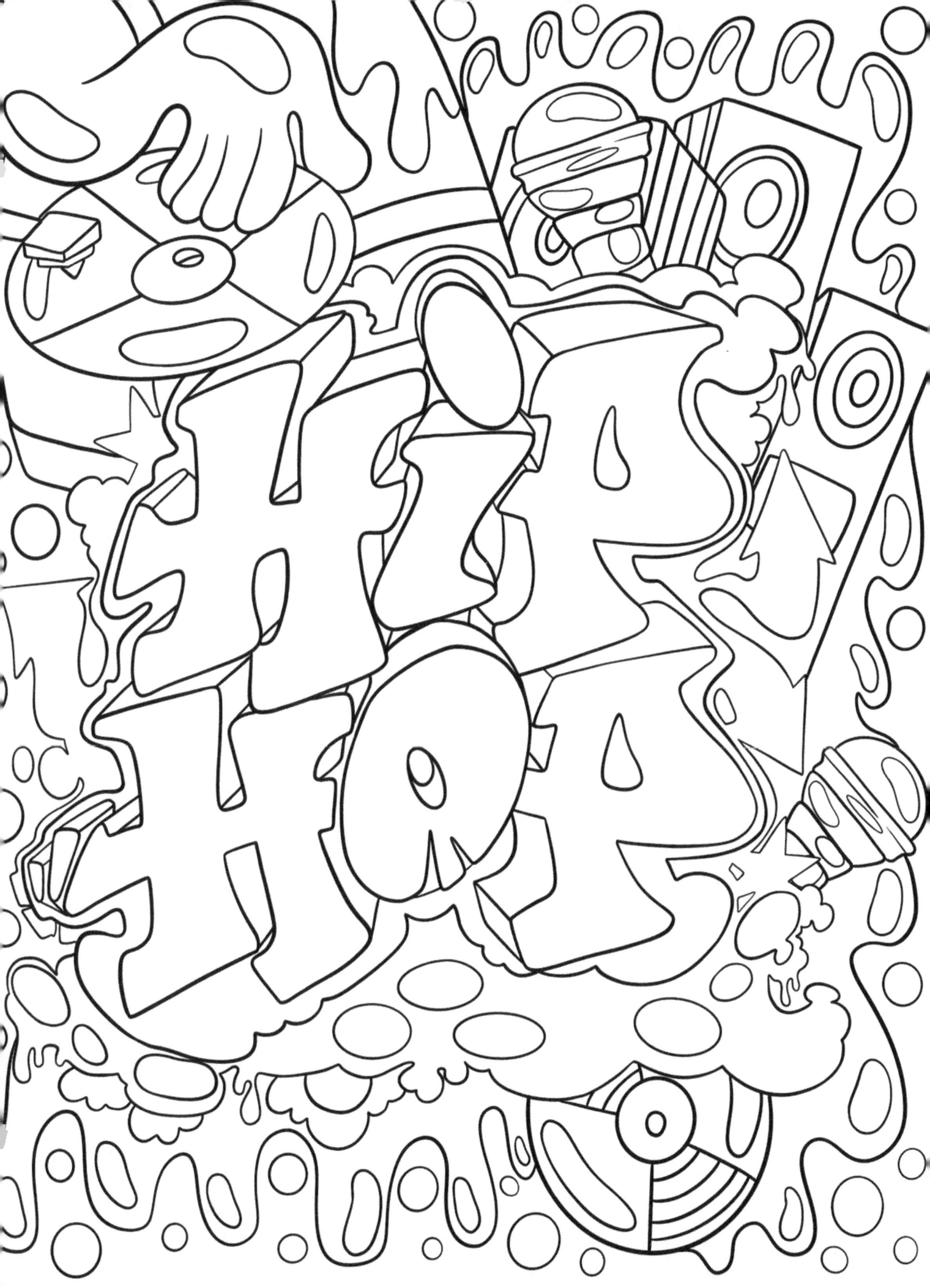

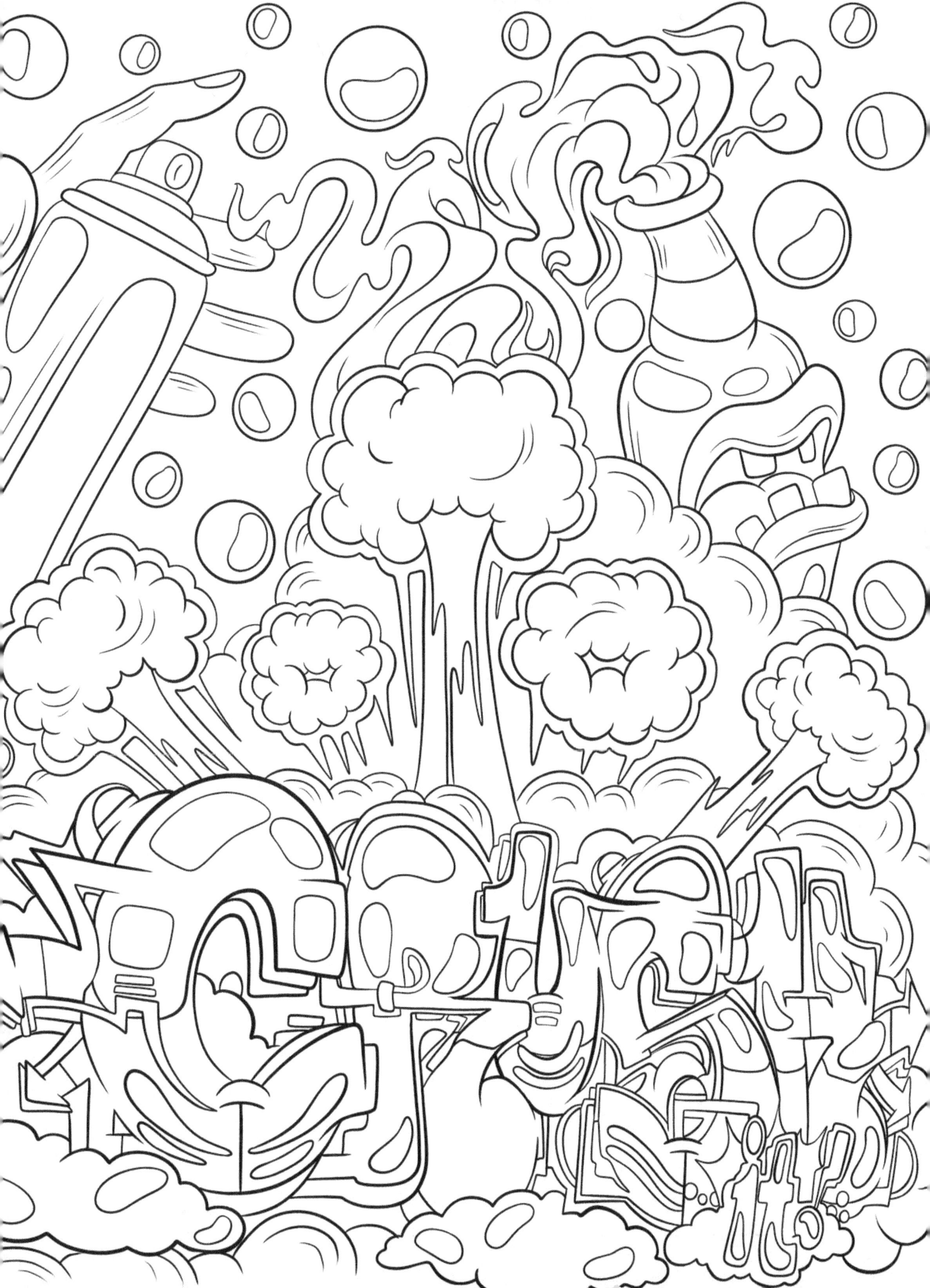

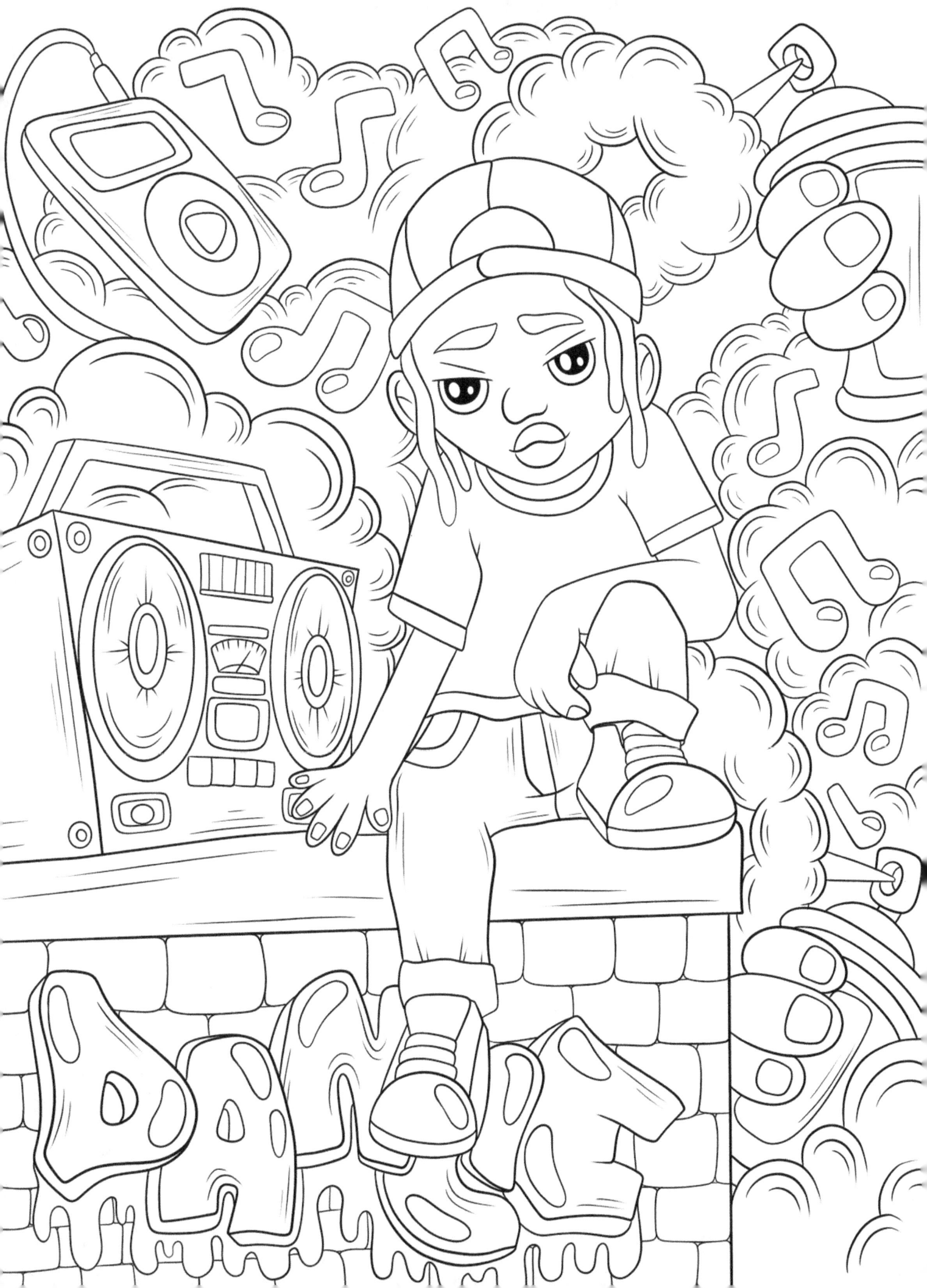

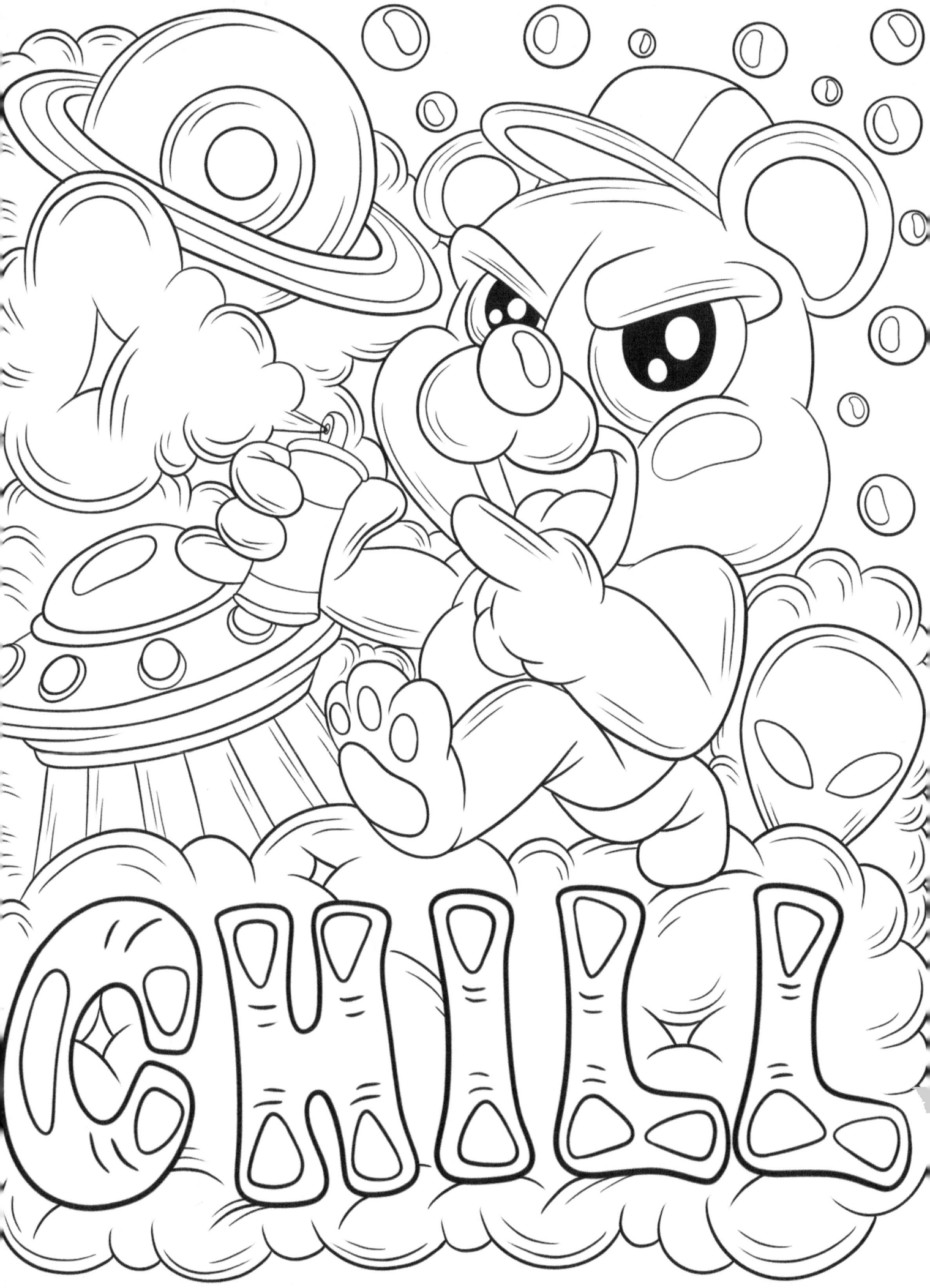

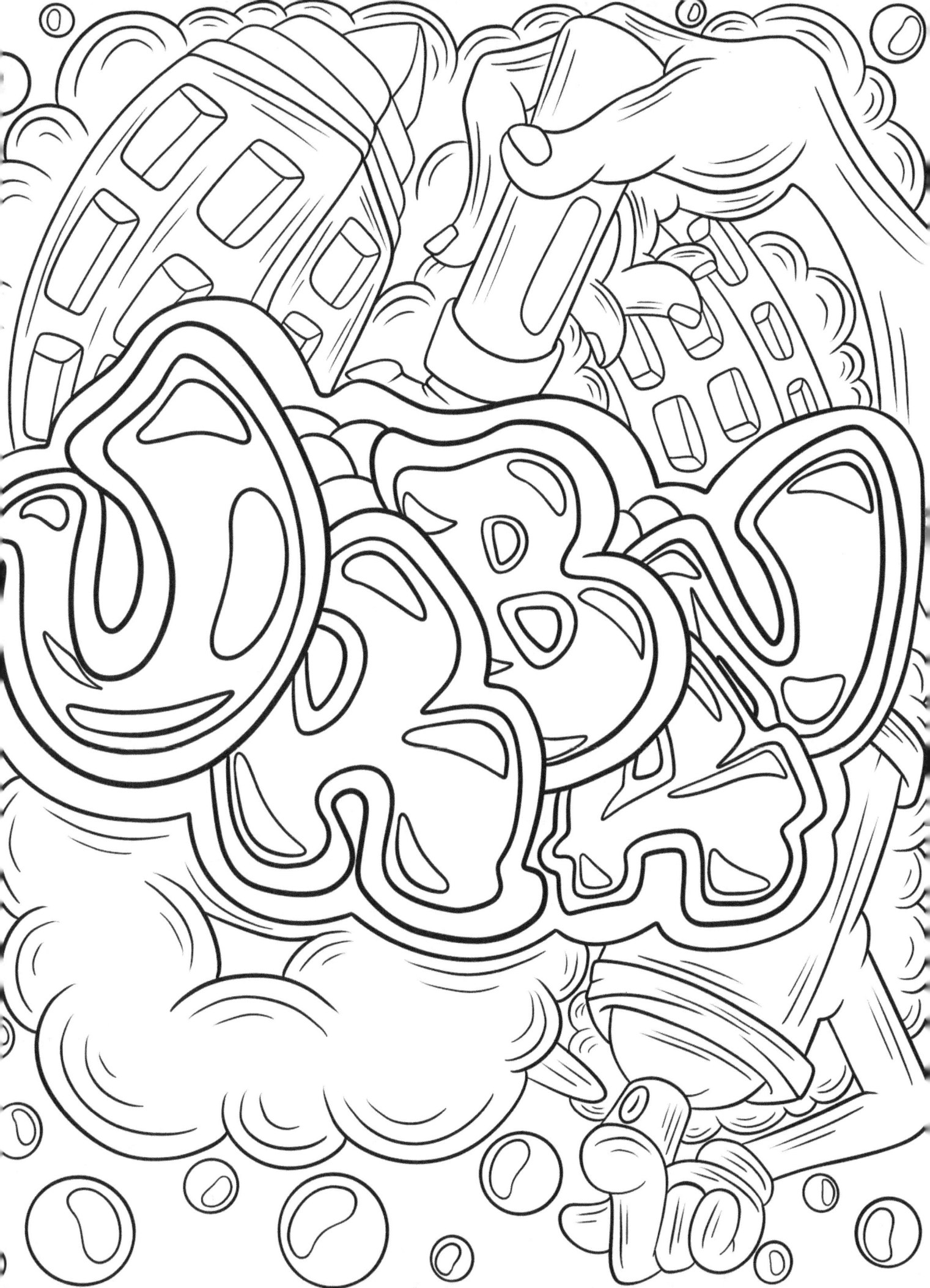

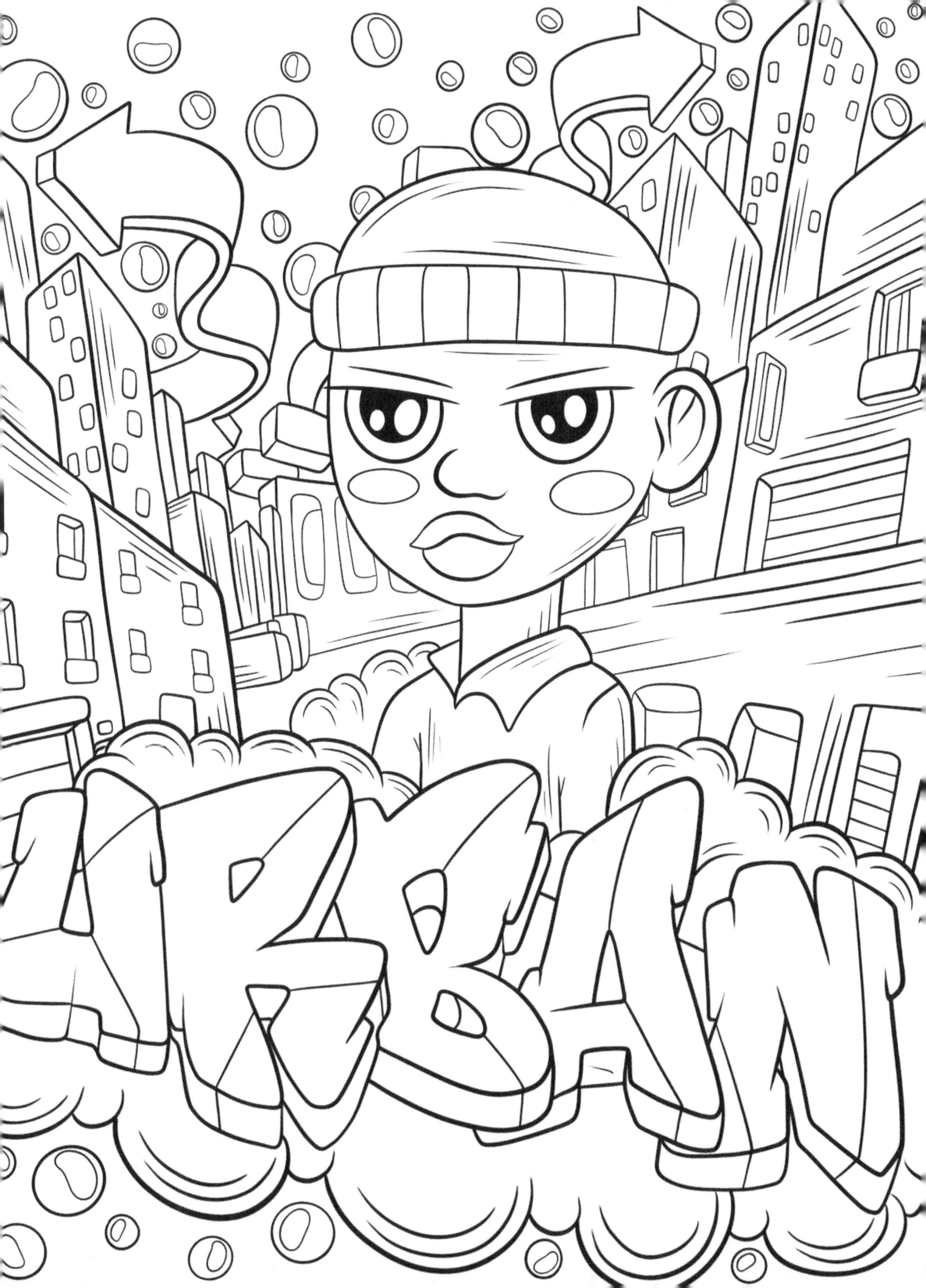

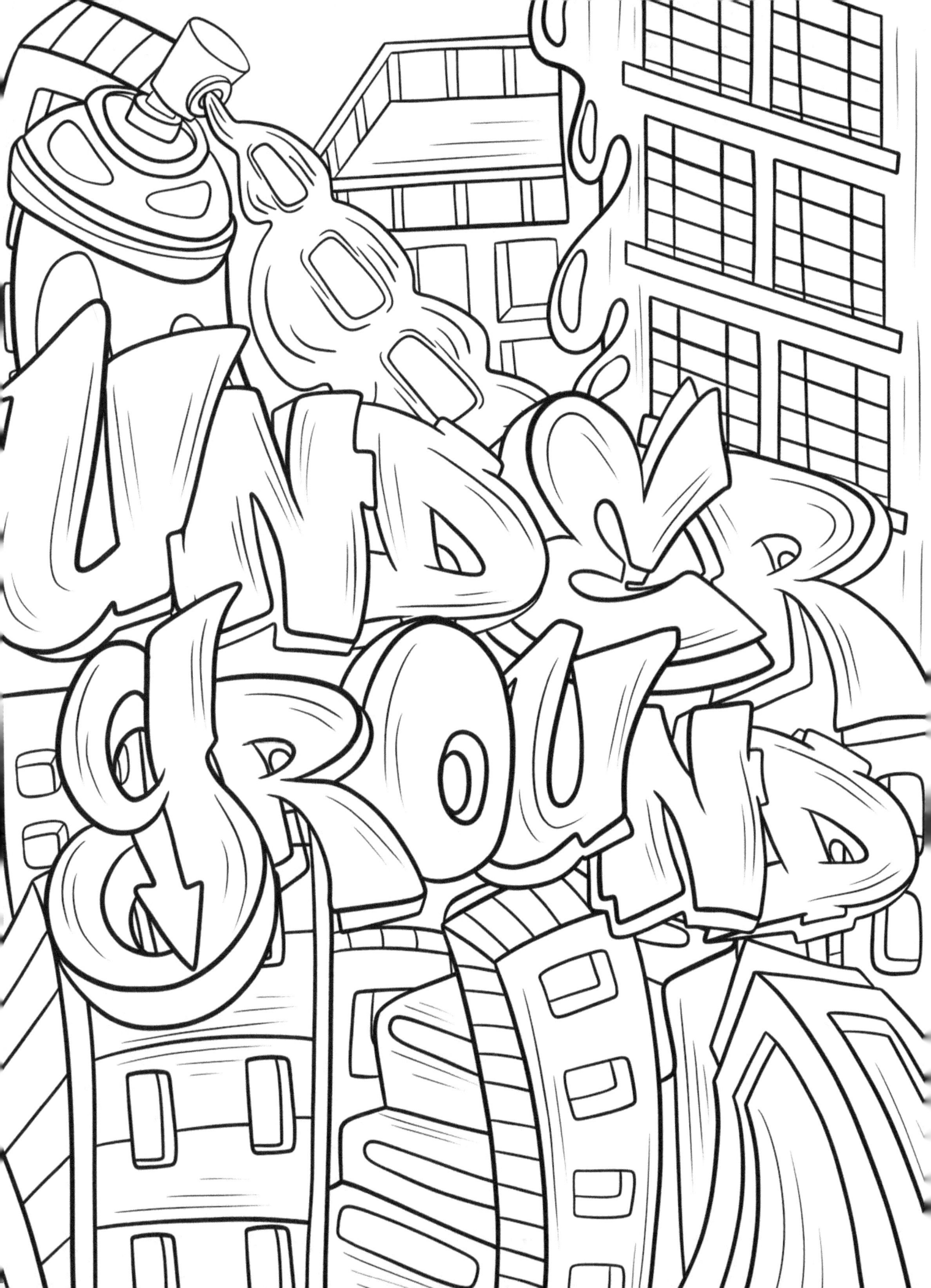

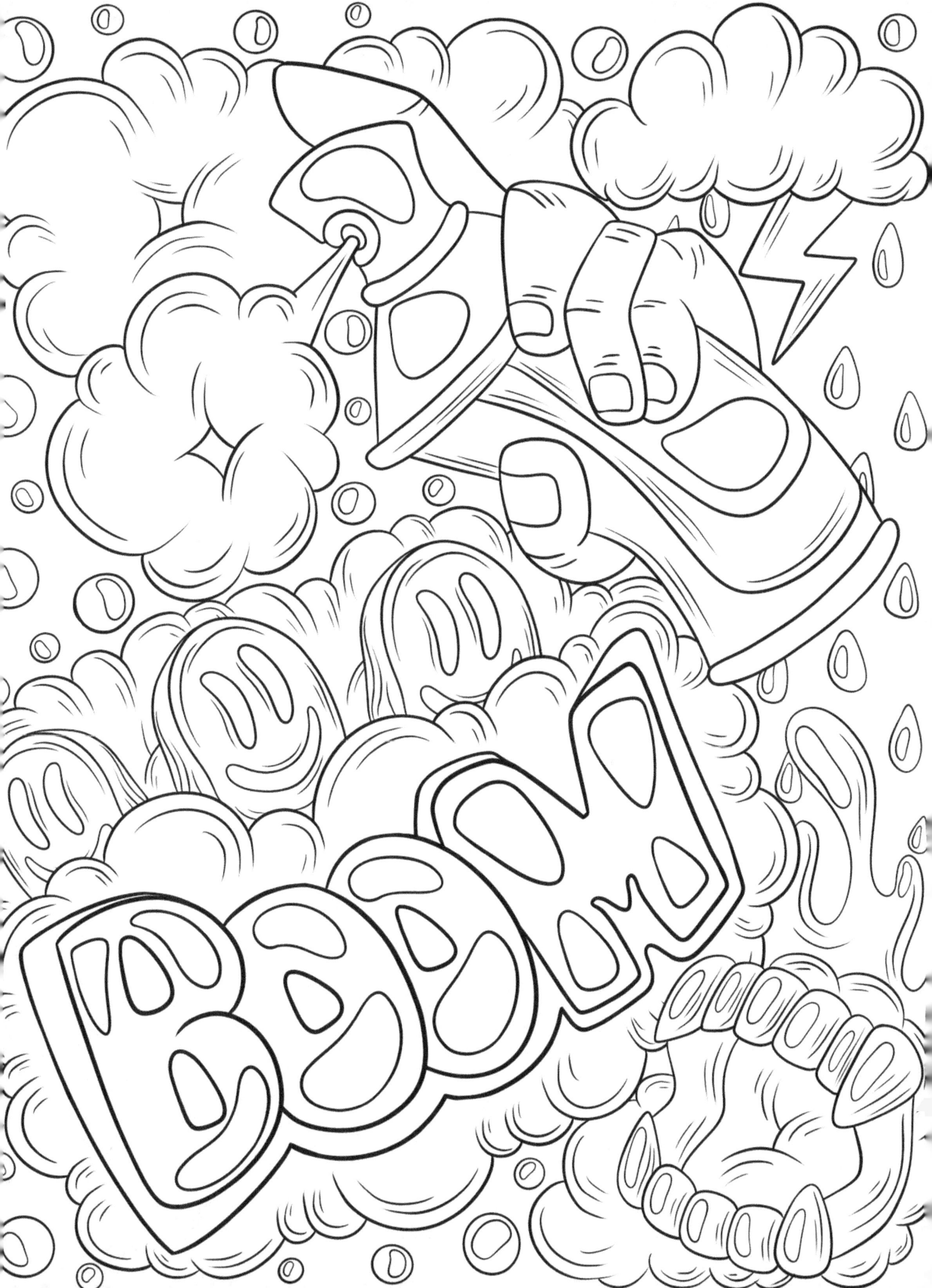

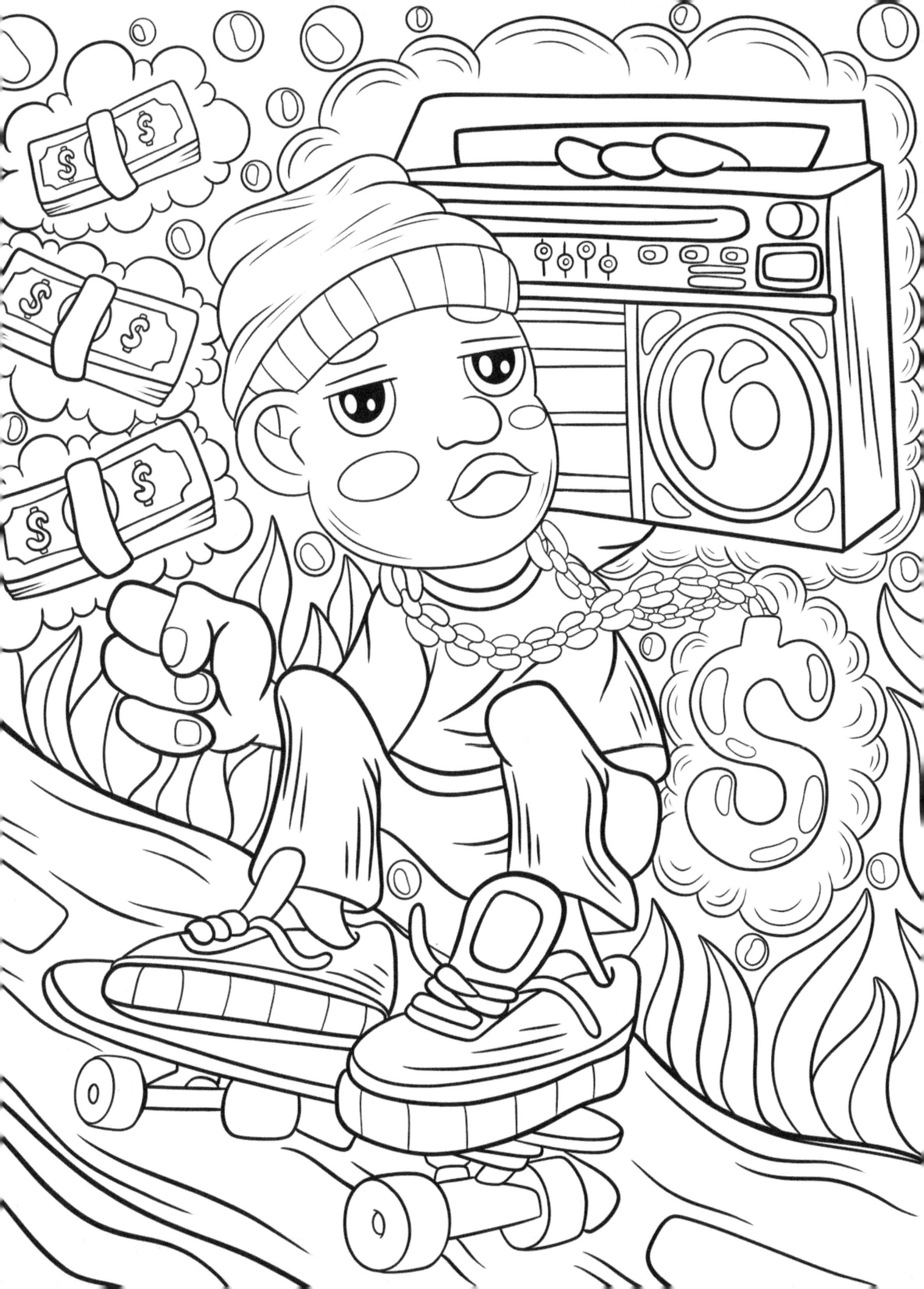

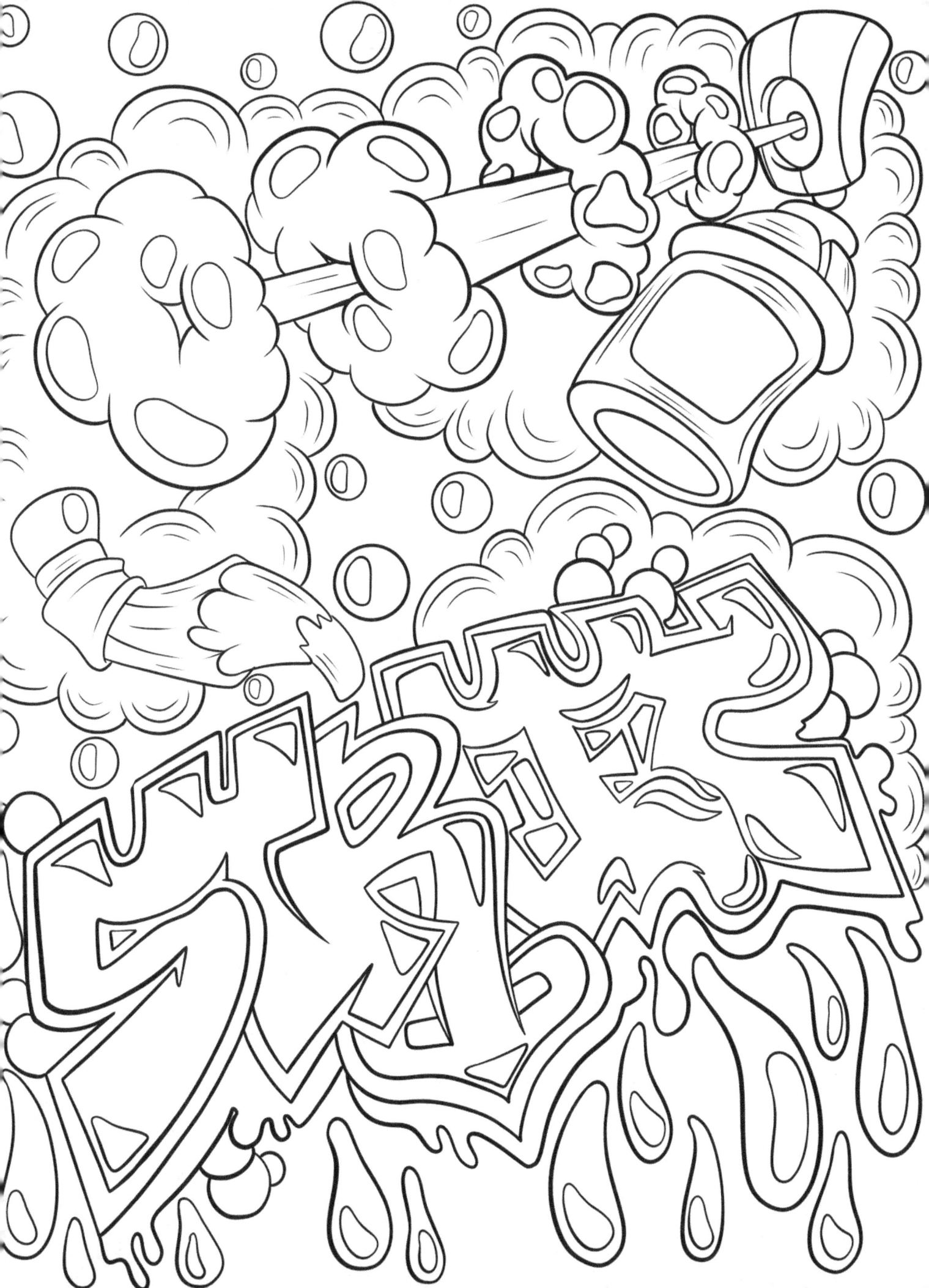

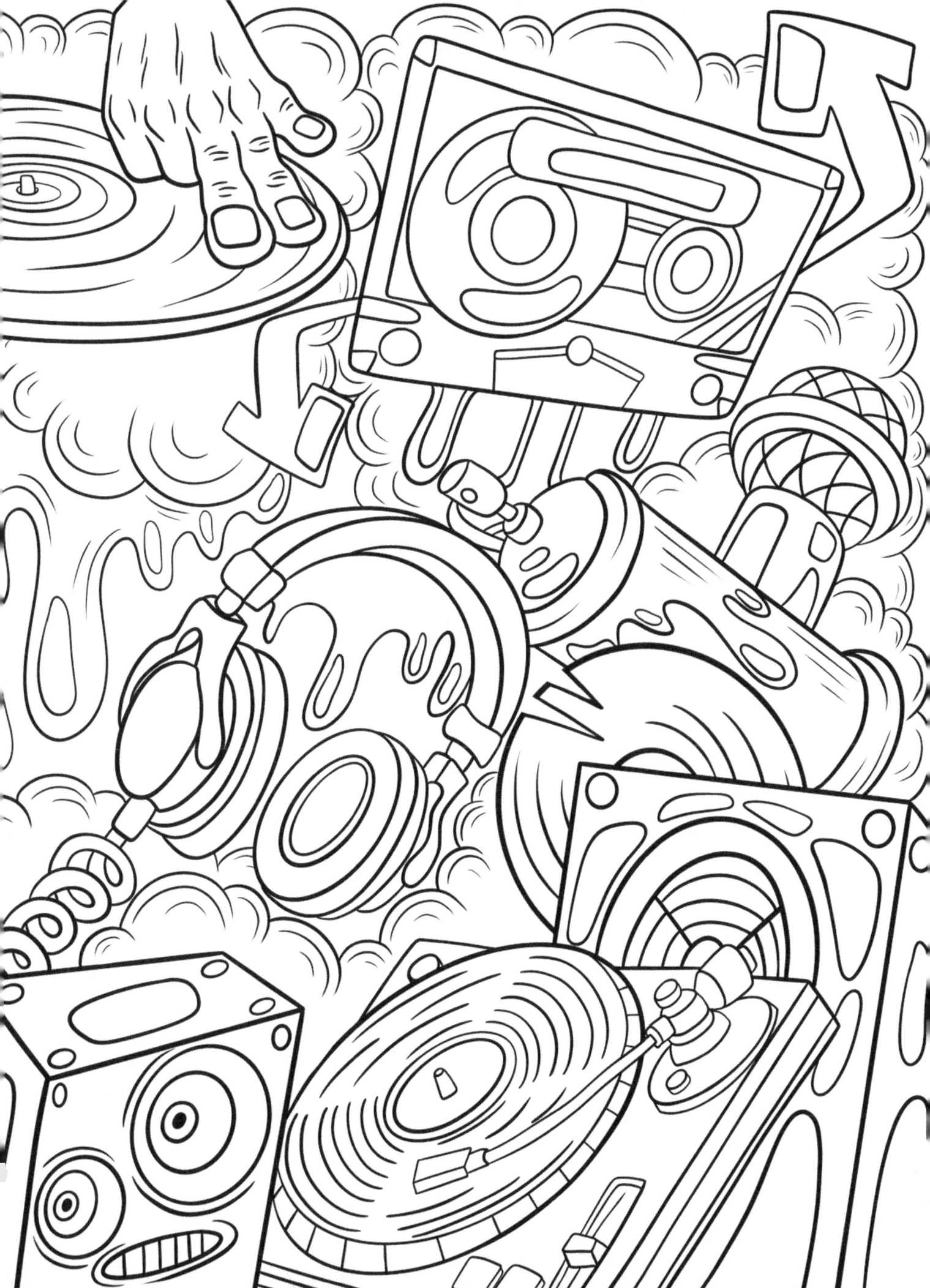

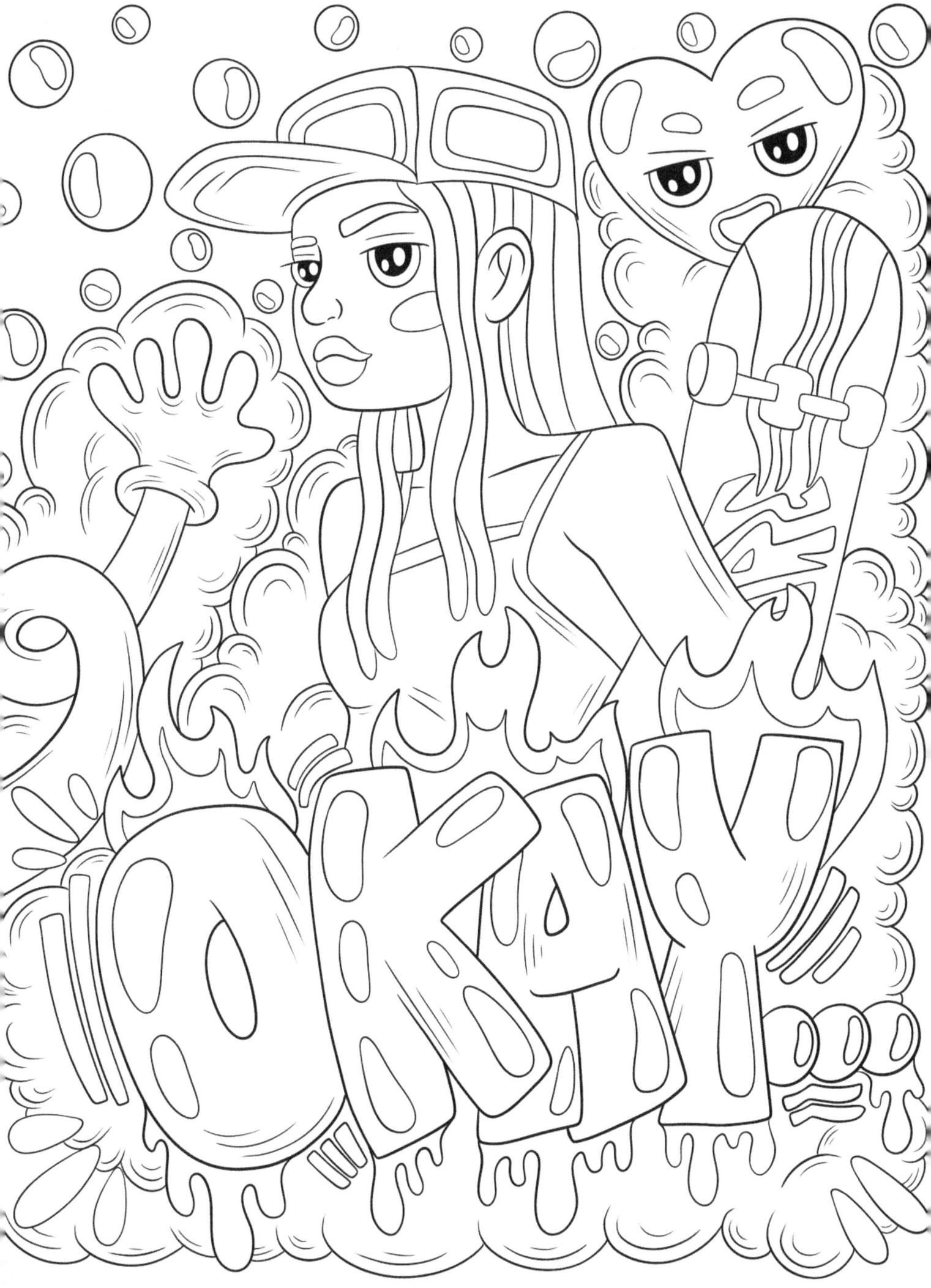

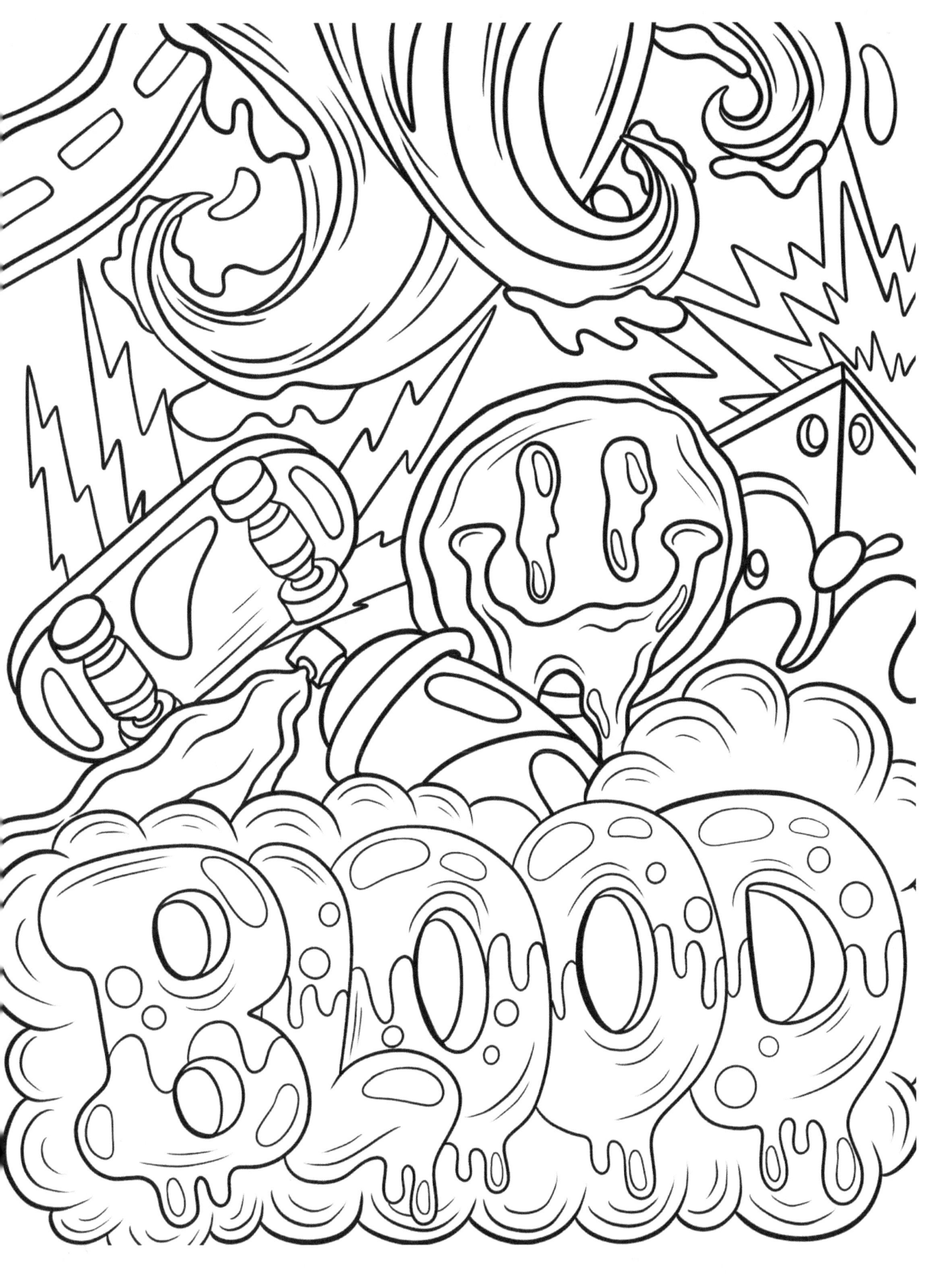

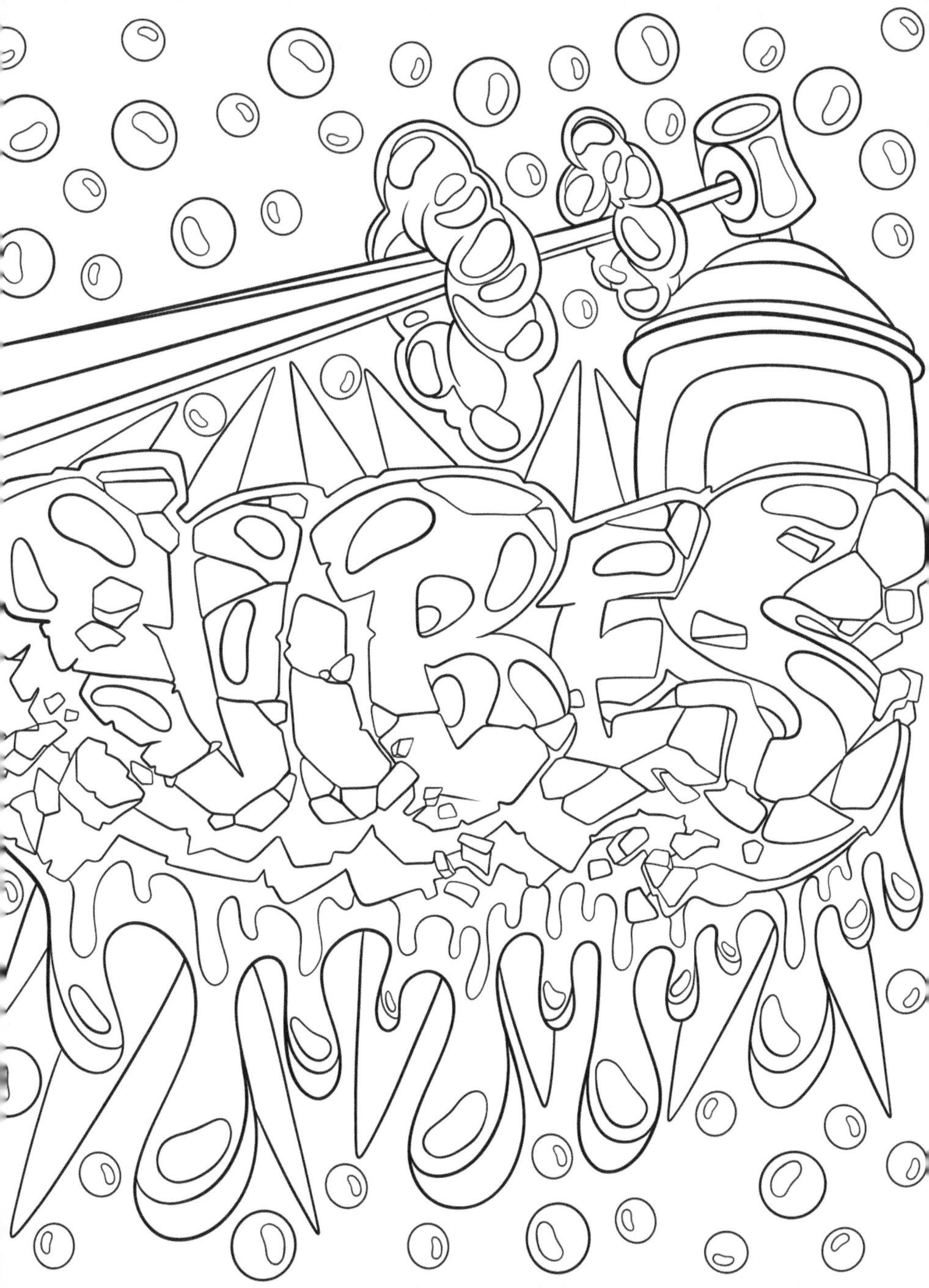

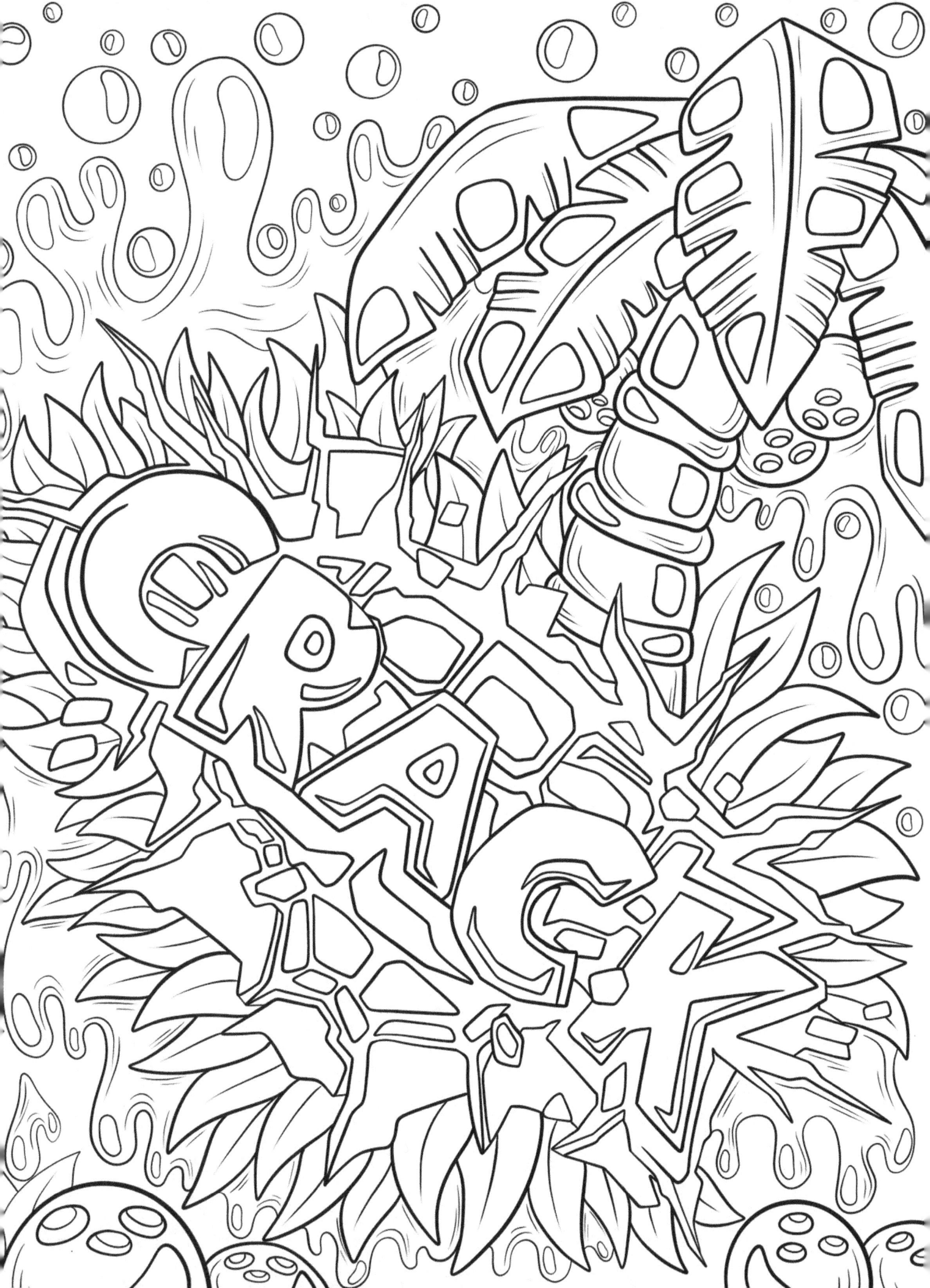

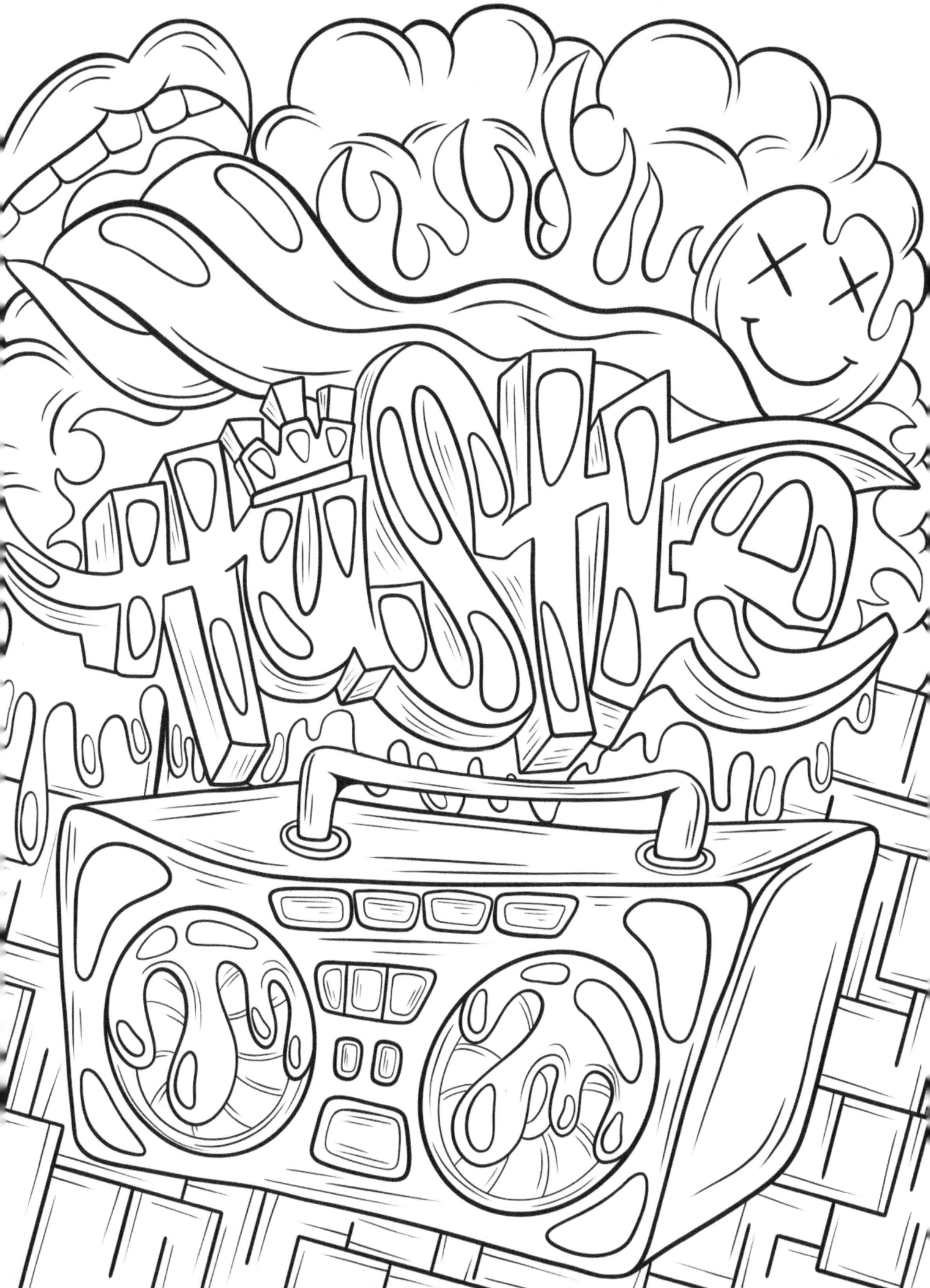

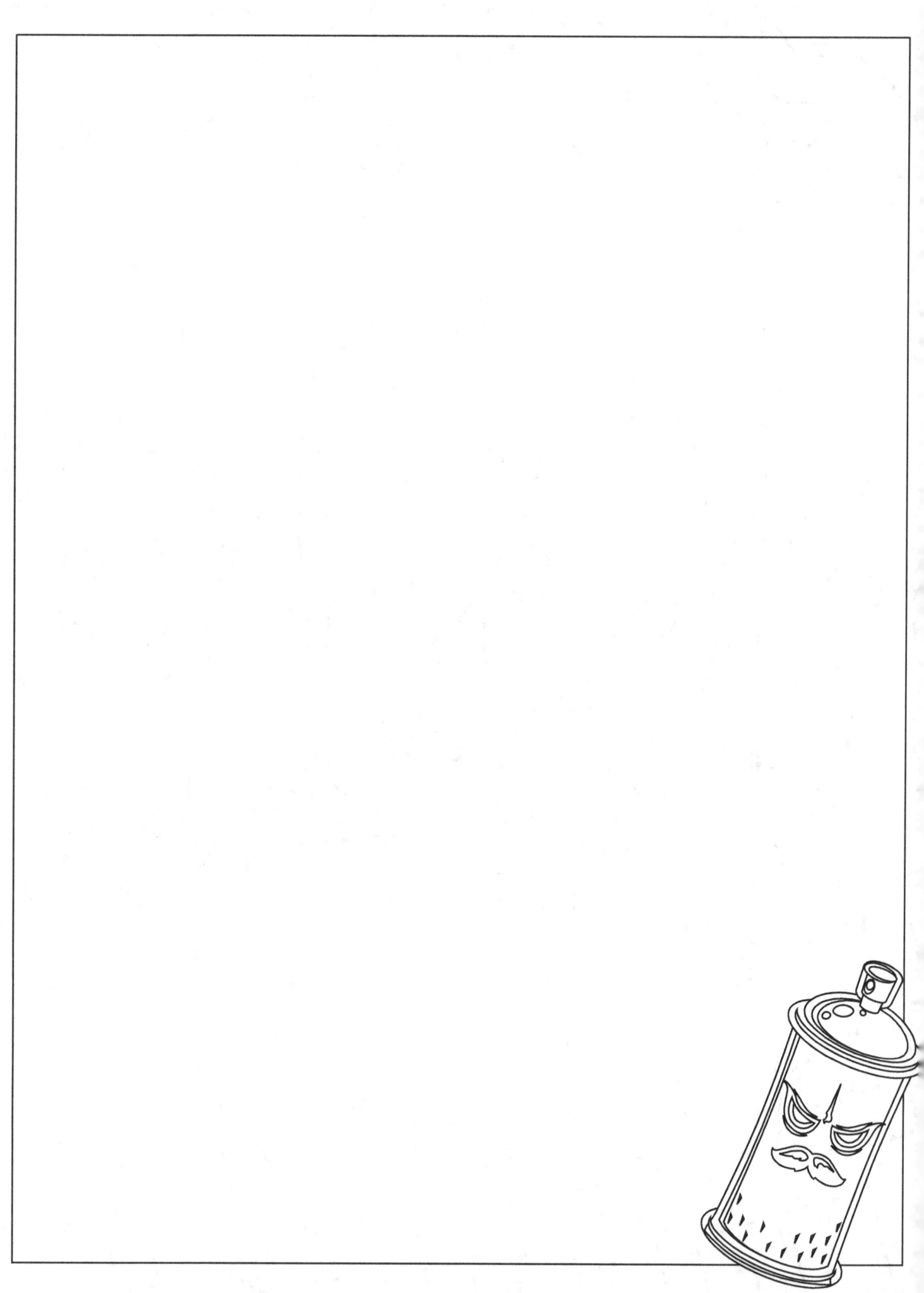

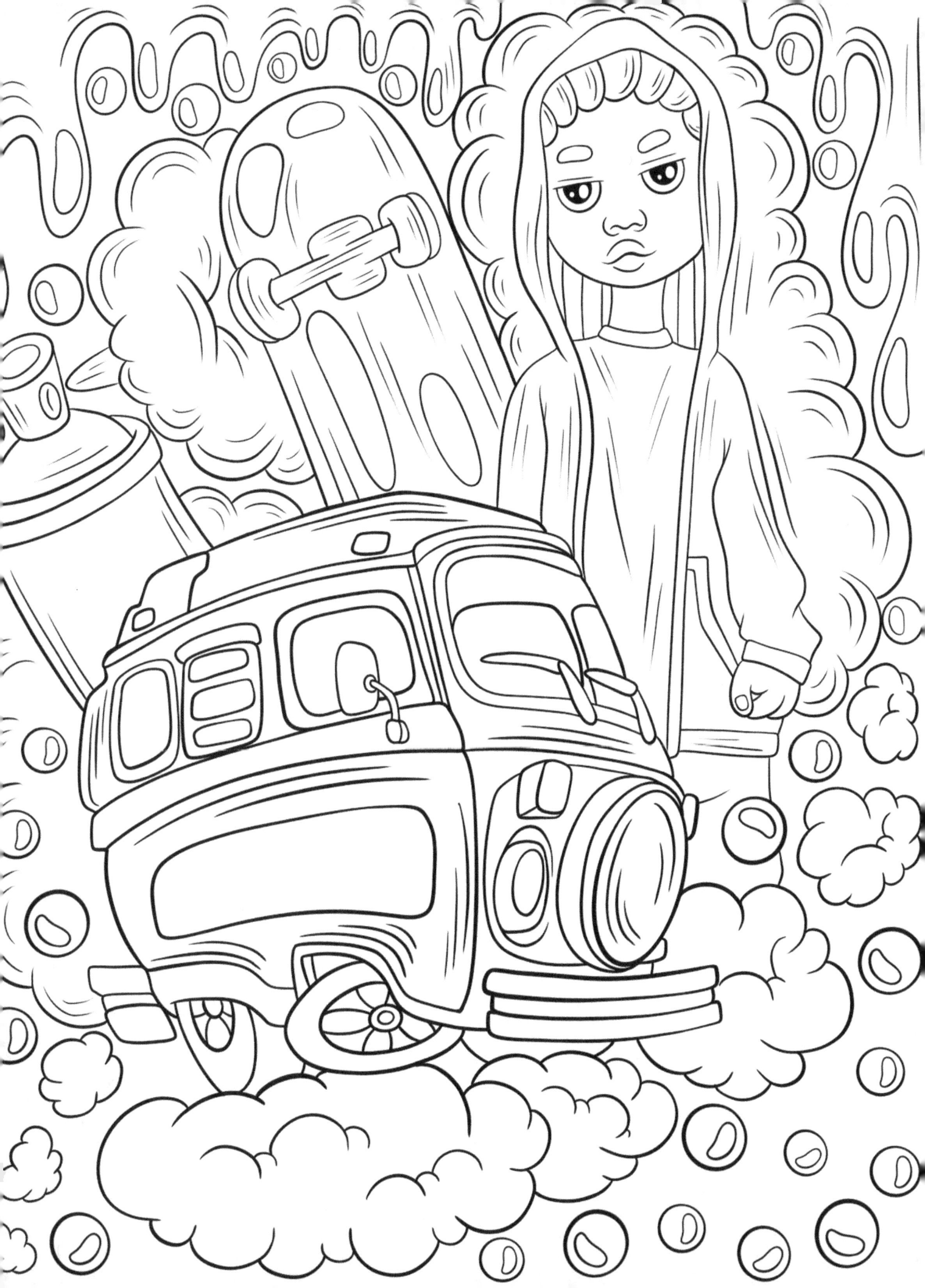

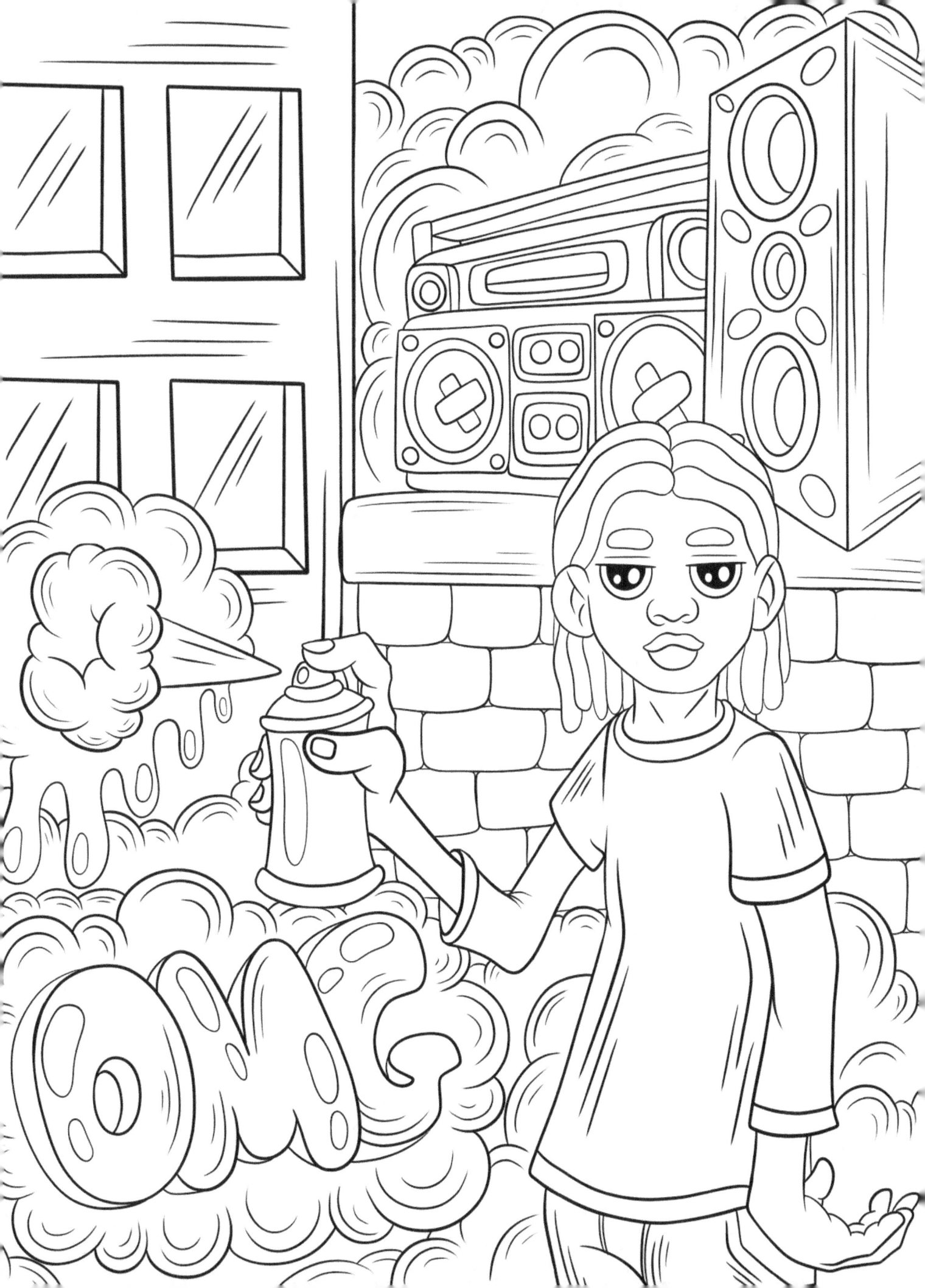

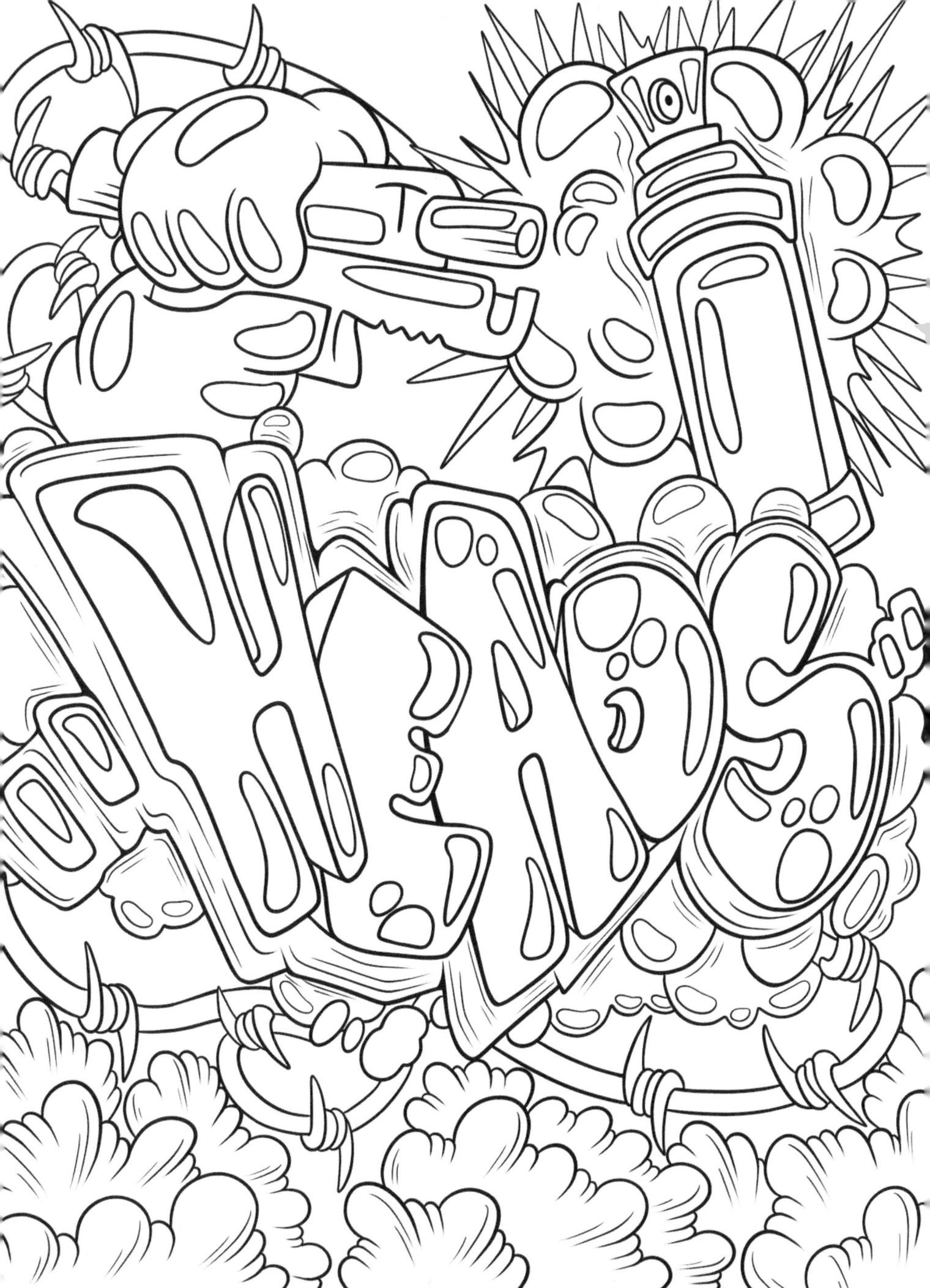

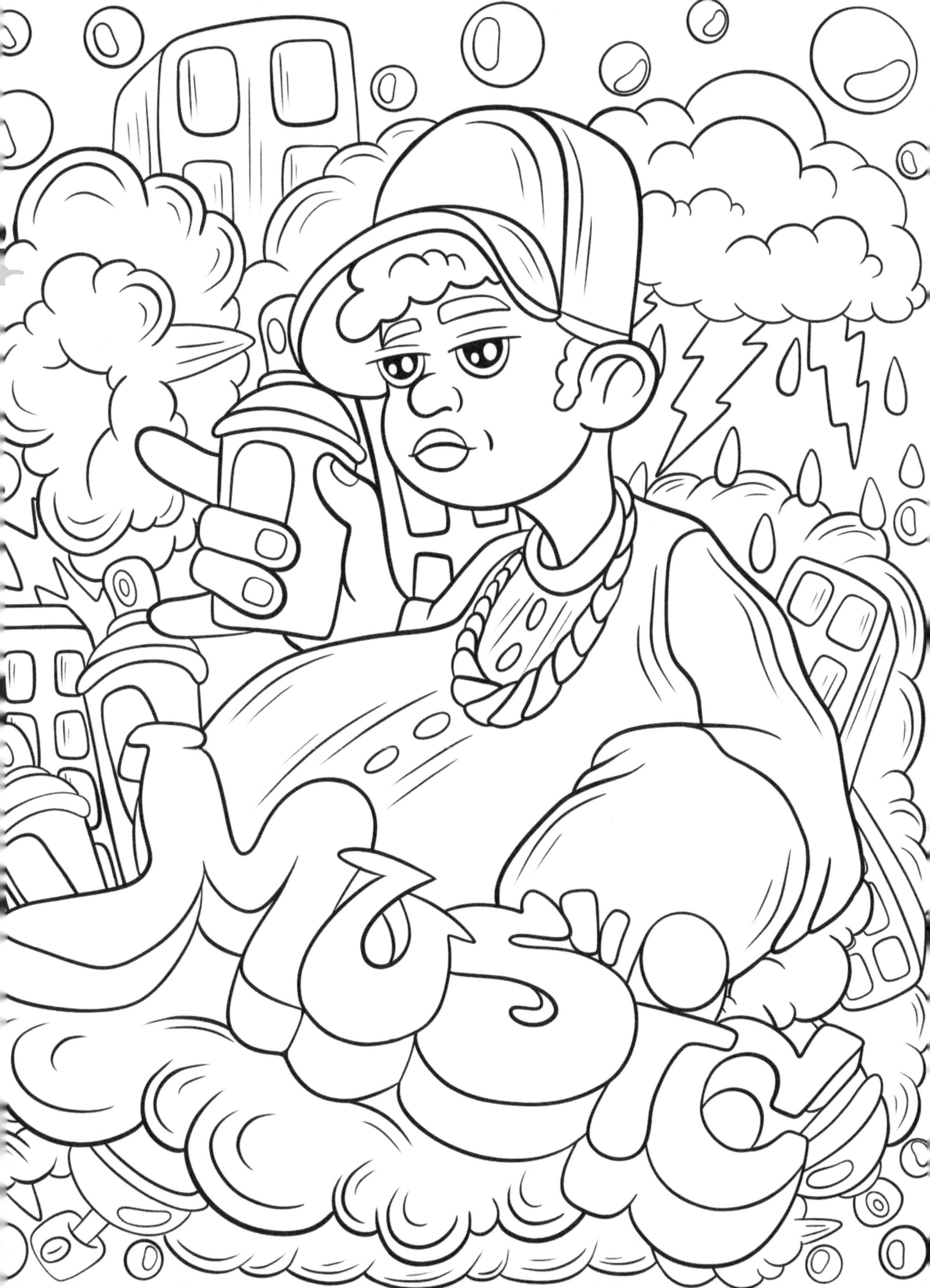

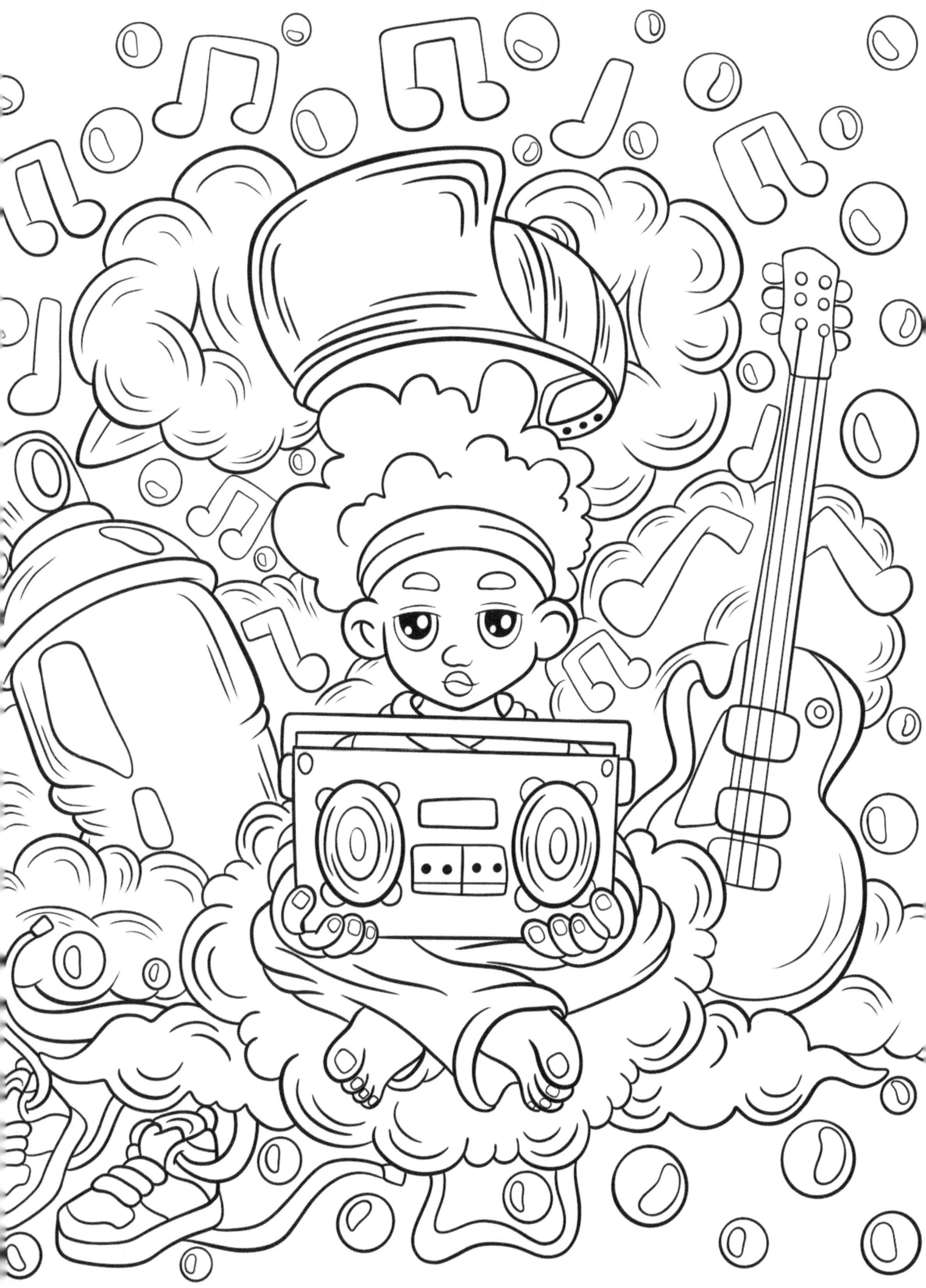

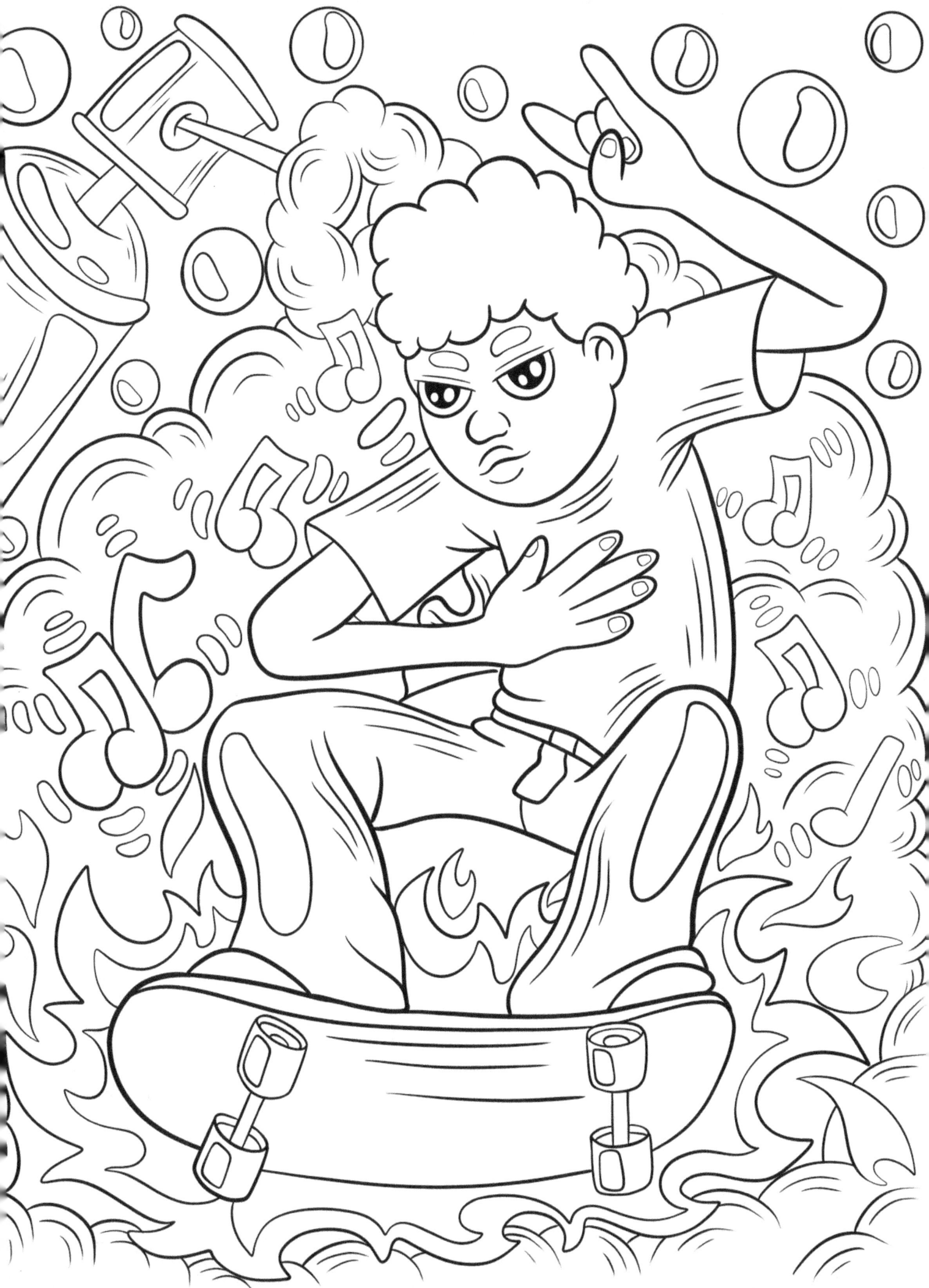

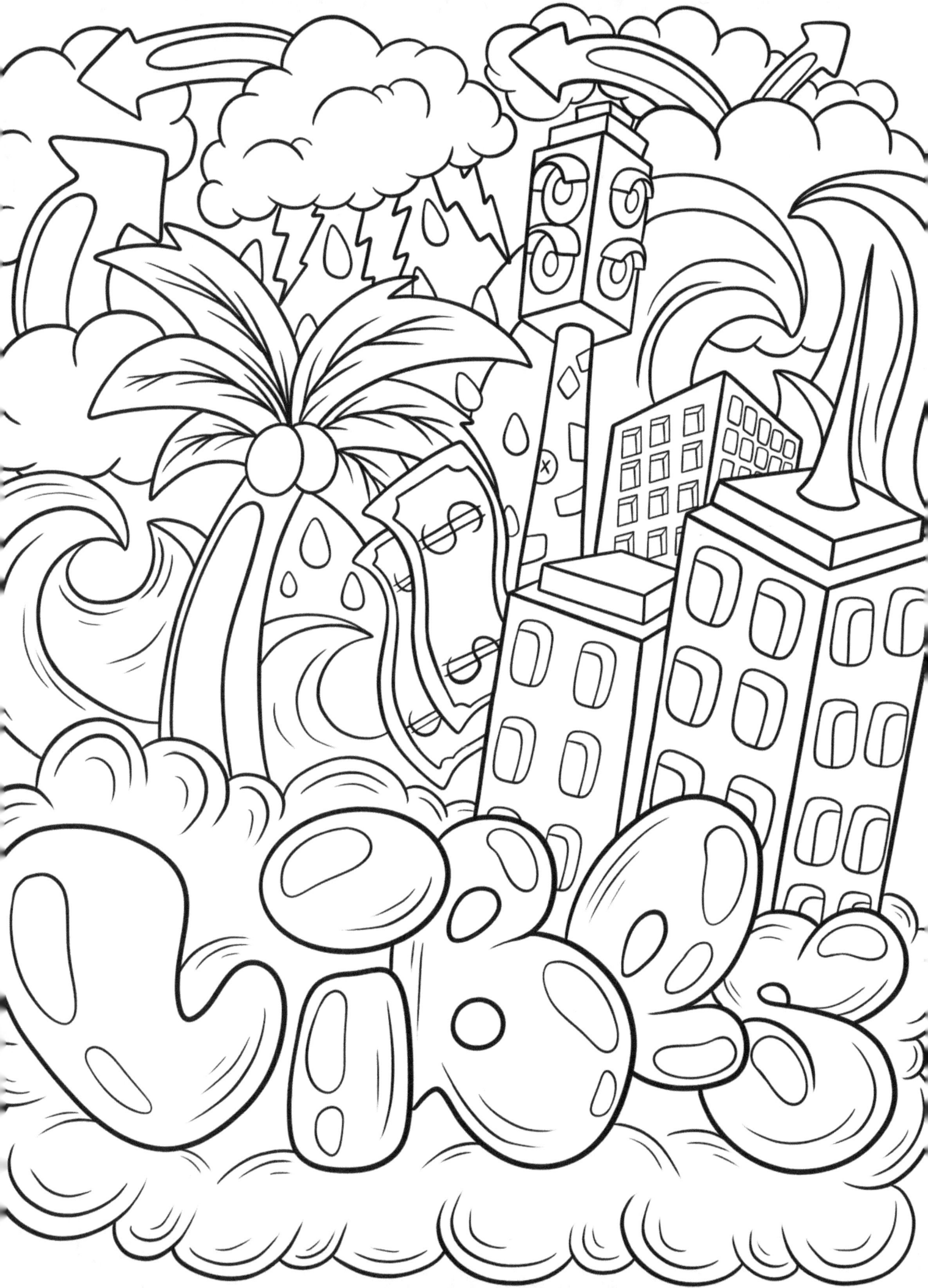

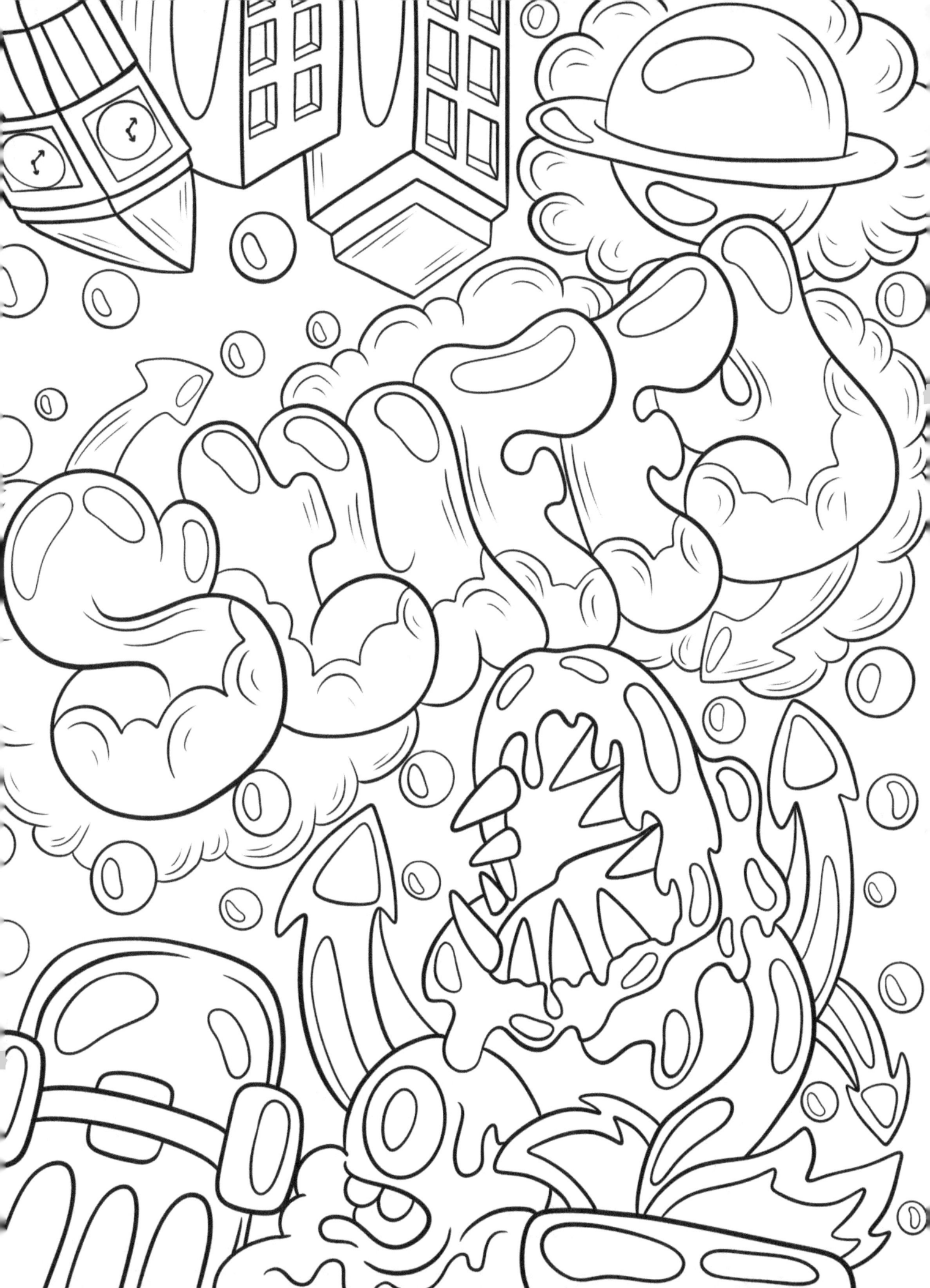

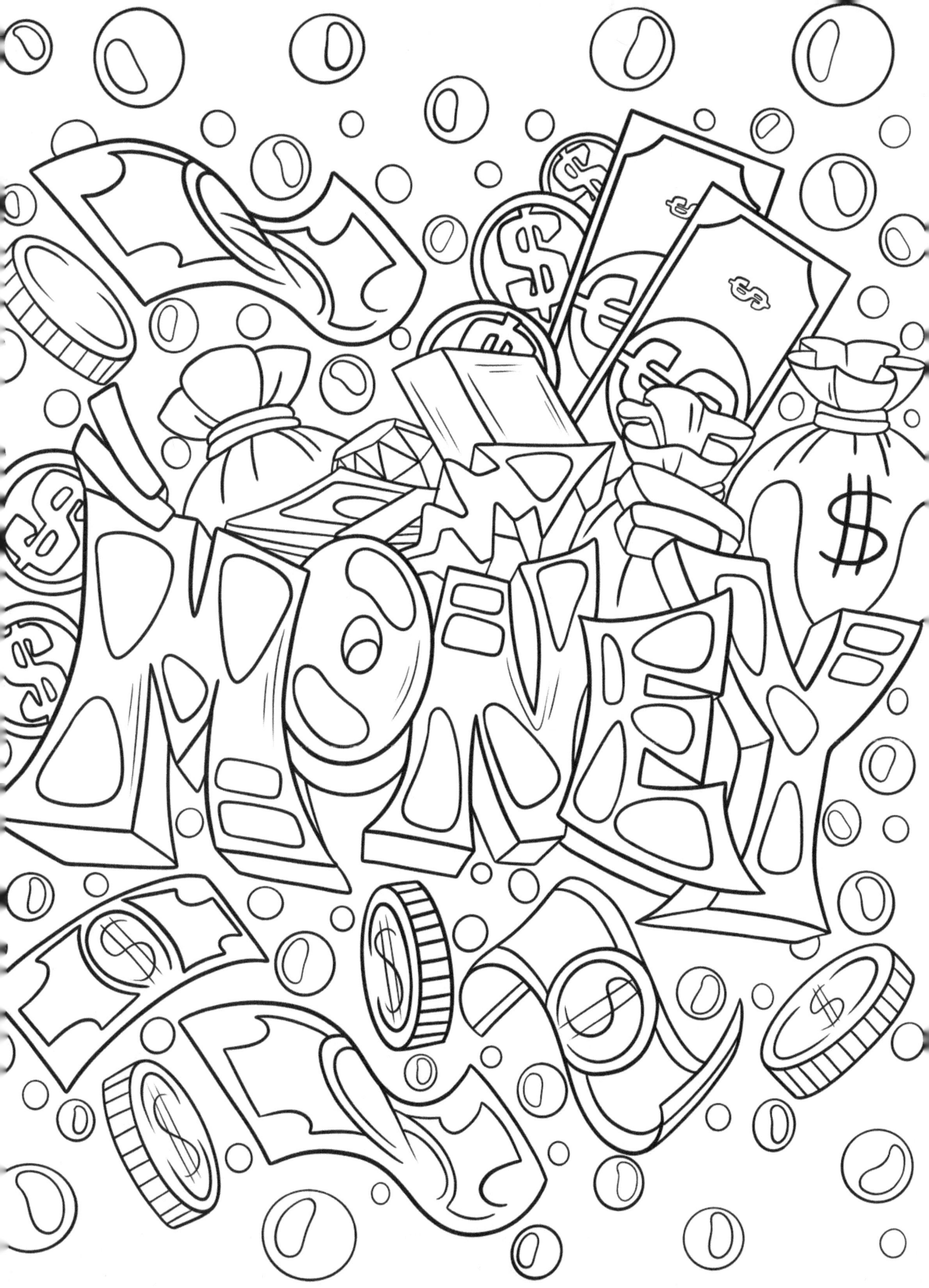

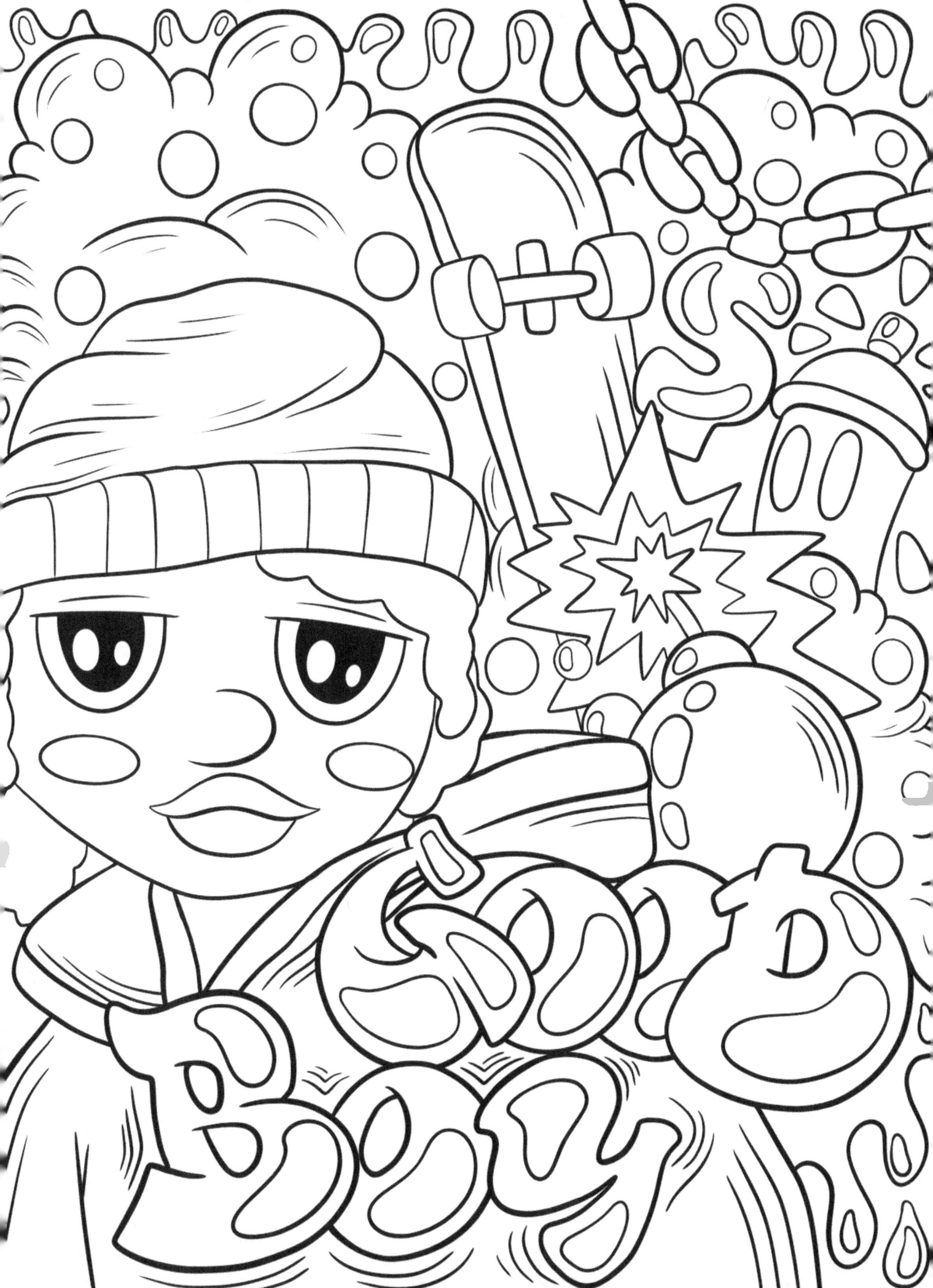

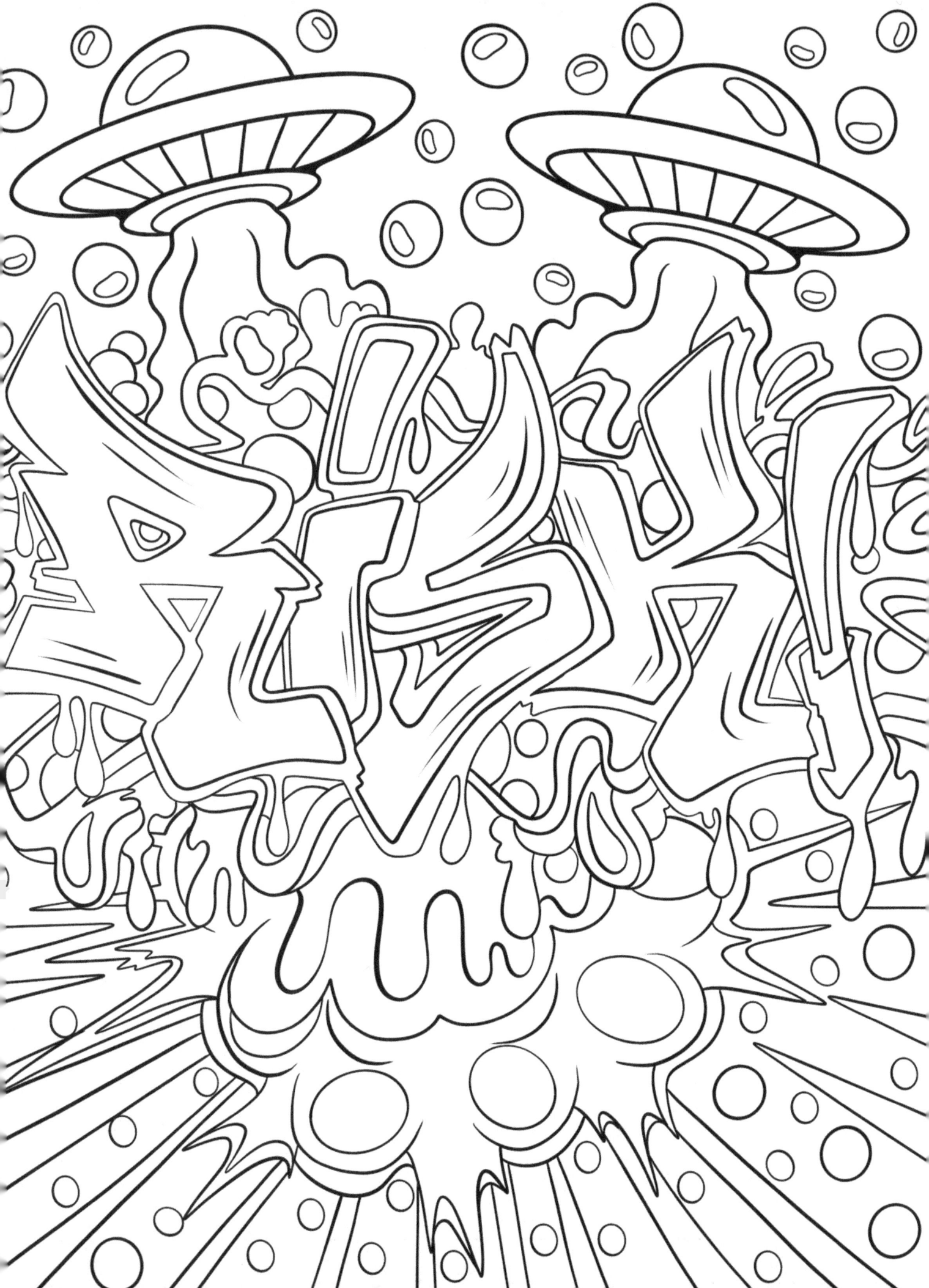

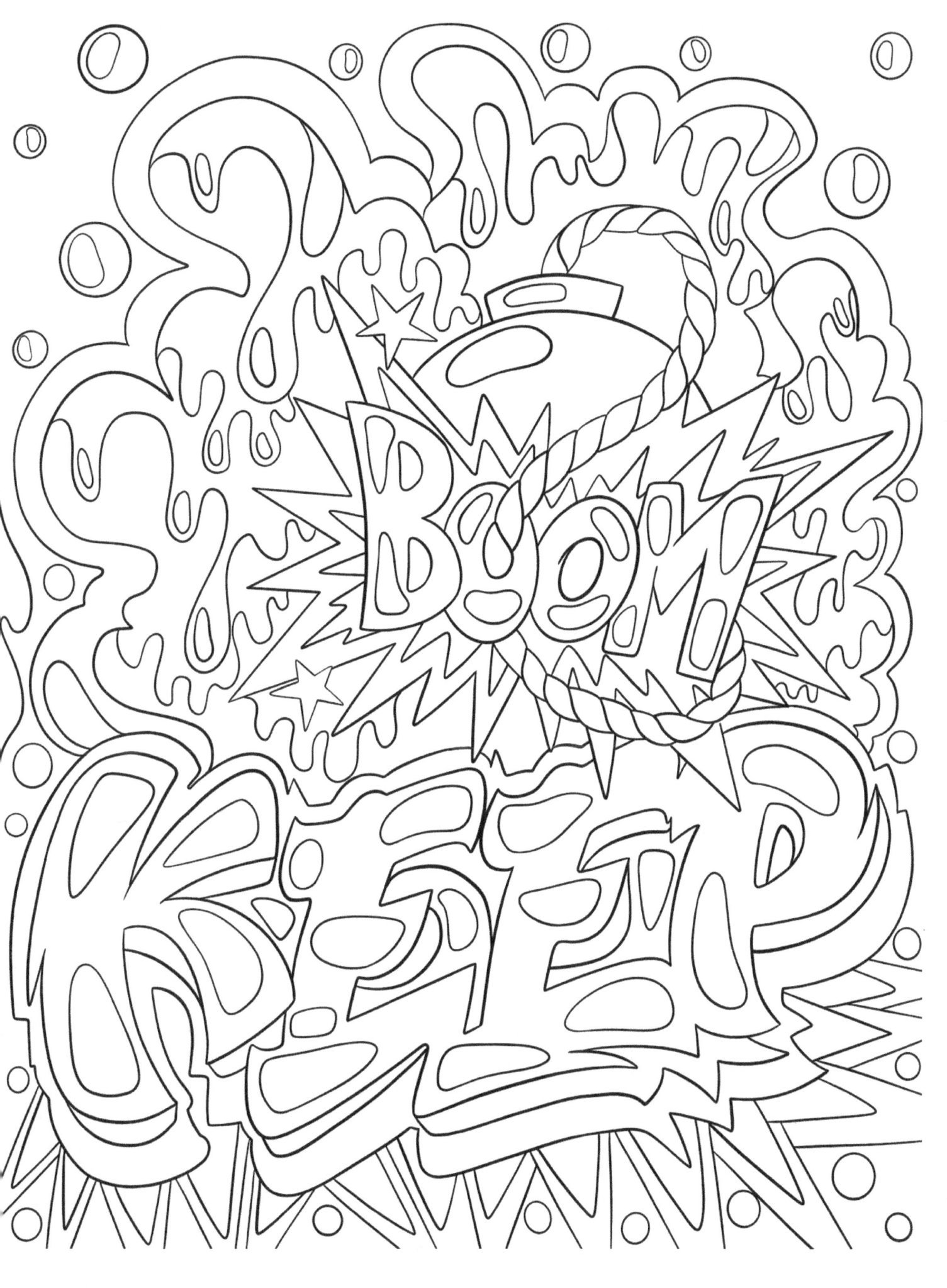

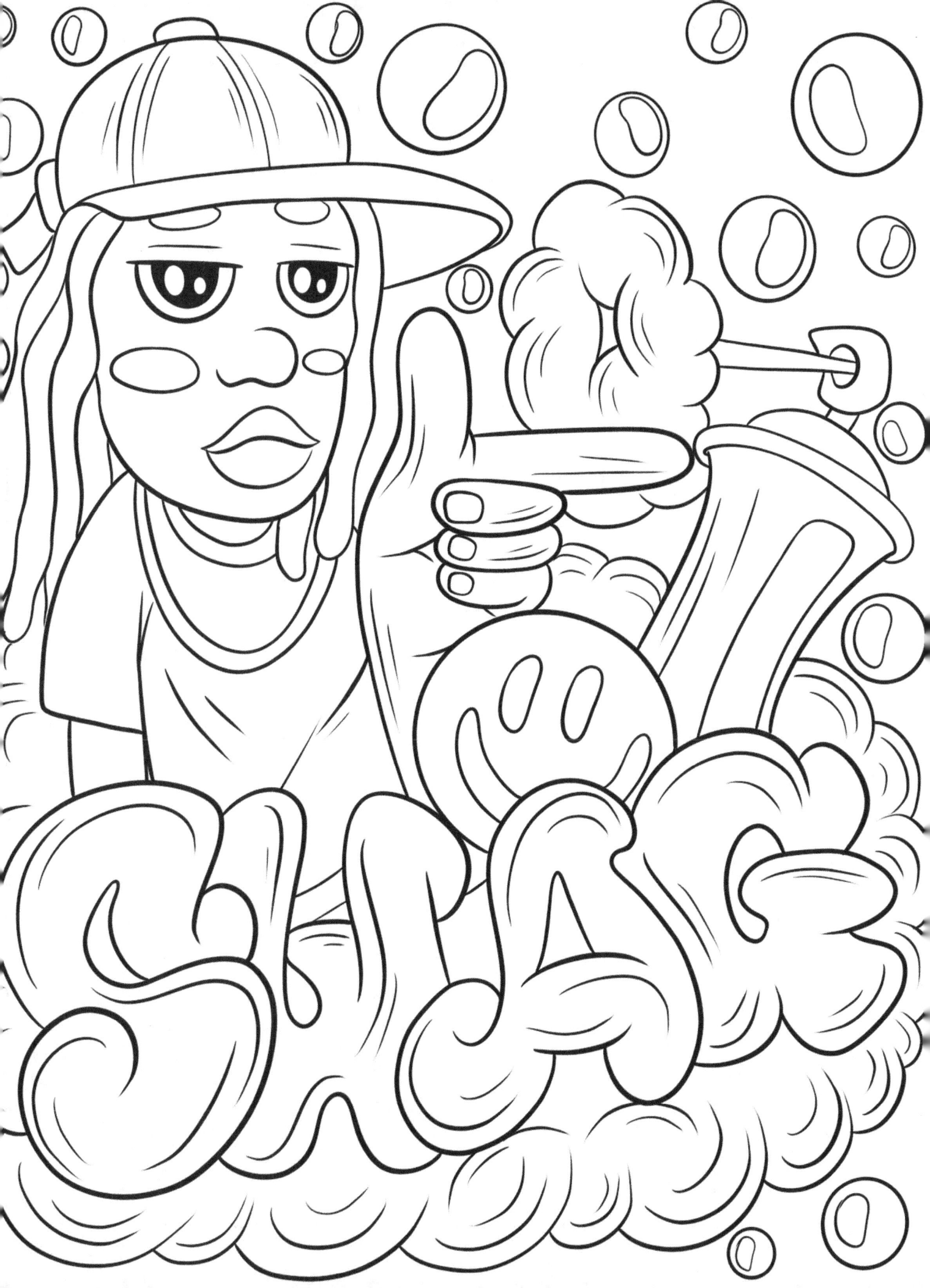

We hope this message finds you well. At Ottmar Karl art
we are dedicated to creating coloring books
that bring joy and relaxation to our customers

If you've had the chance to explore our coloring books and enjoyed the experience
we would be incredibly grateful if you could take a moment to share your thoughts with us
Your feedback is invaluable and helps us improve our products

LEAVE A REVIEW AND LET US KNOW

What coloring book did you try ?
What aspects did you enjoy the most ?
How did it contribute to your relaxation or creative moments ?

Your insights will not only encourage our team but also assist
other coloring enthusiasts in making informed decisions

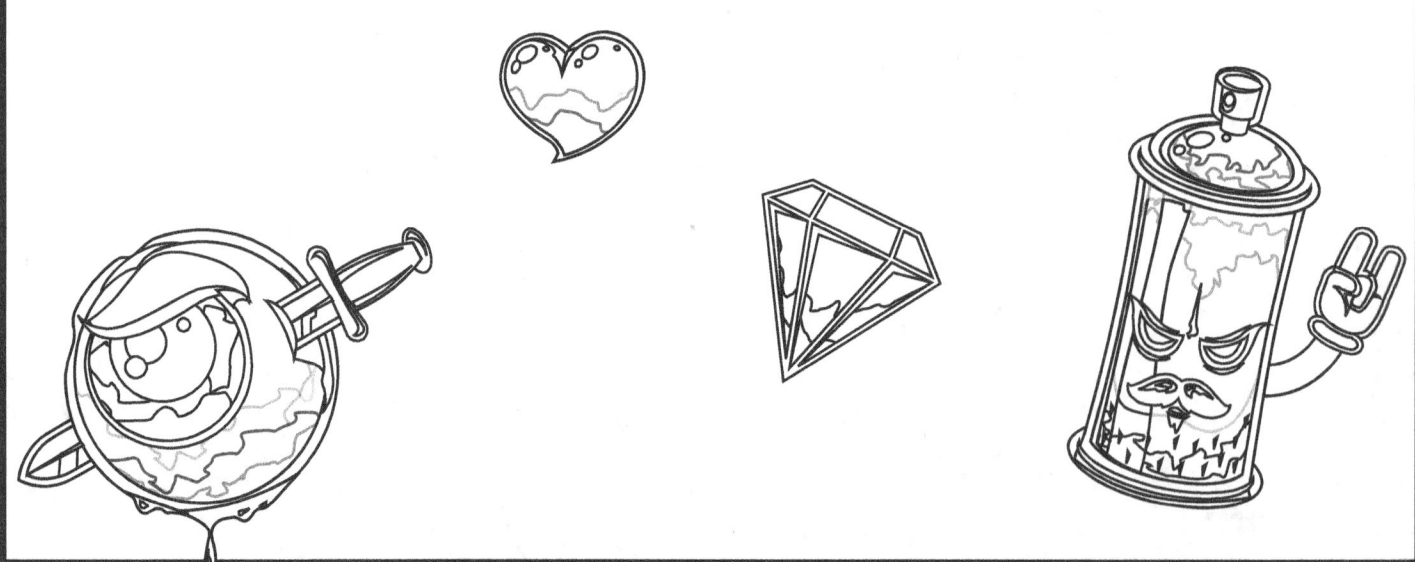